JÜRGEN LEWANDOWSKI

WITH CONTRIBUTIONS
FROM TOBIAS AICHELE
AND WOLFGANG BLAUBE

THE
ROOTS
OF
A LEGEND

PORSCHE 901

DELIUS KLASING VERLAG

CONTENTS

FOREWORD

DR. WOLFGANG
PORSCHE

The Porsche 911 is a legend – a sculpture that, for half a century, has been inspiring its owners and bringing them untold pleasure, while chalking up thousands of victories on race tracks the world over. And when I look at an early 911 today, I never cease to be amazed by the aesthetics of the lines and the perfection of the form created by my late elder brother Ferdinand Alexander – there can be very few cars indeed that have lost nothing of their original quality over such a long period of time. The 911 is a true gem that appears to link seamlessly to the 356, reinforcing its qualities and taking the concept of the air-cooled, rear-mounted engine to a whole new level, and that ultimately brought long-term survival to the Porsche name.

What seems in retrospect so very natural was in reality an extremely arduous process that spanned many years and put those responsible through a rollercoaster ride of emotions. There were endless discussions on the wheelbase and the size of the interior – and the form, too, was by no means a stroke of genius that simply fell from the skies. The timeless design of the 901 succeeded in retaining the elegance of the 356 Coupe, while carrying forward the identity of the unique Porsche design language. And it did so with an enduring success that is impressively evidenced by the now seven generations of the 911 model range.

The transition from the 356 to the 901 has never before been documented as precisely as this – it is the purpose of this book to shed more light on this exceptional period; to describe the genesis of the 901. It offers a new perspective of the brand and the transition from constructor of sporty vehicles based on the VW Beetle to the creator of its very own genre of sports cars. This book goes to the very heart of the Porsche brand – to the creation of the 901, which rapidly transformed into the 911.

Wolfgang Porsche

TIMES ARE CHANGING

There can be very few cars on which so many books have been written as the Porsche 911. This speaks not only to the importance and appeal of this exceptional sports car, but also to its capacity to inspire so many authors. It also bears testimony to the openness of Porsche itself and its willingness to provide access to its archive. However, while all those books published to date have devoted a remarkable degree of detail to the development of this most definitive of sports cars, there has been very little to speak of written about the period that saw Dr. Ing. h.c. F. Porsche KG transform from the much-respected producer of a VW Beetle derivative to the manufacturer of a completely independent sports car that had not one single screw in common with the 356. This successor, bearing the designation 901, may have come as something of a surprise to the outside world, but the internal ruminations and deliberations on this car had been lengthy – lengthier than most observers might imagine.

The route traveled to the 901 at the end of the 1950s was not an easy one for those involved because the 356 was still selling well – and, in parallel, there was still no final decision on whether or not to stick with a pure two-seater. By opting for a 2+2-seater, the path to a Porsche that could also be used by the whole family would basically be blocked for some considerable time. And who could possibly know in these post-war years whether there would be enough money in the world over a long enough timeframe for something as luxurious as a sports car? Those were fraught times, during which a family had the courage to embark upon a whole new adventure – an adventure that could just as easily have brought them to ruin.

It was a time of enormous change – for both the family and industry. It was a time in which the Porsche 901 was also an object of transition – that may not have been the plan, but it was certainly the outcome. The now so familiar 911 would probably have launched its global career just as well under the 901 nameplate, but, for reasons that will be explained later, it was not to be. As a result, the 901 has always remained something of a mystery – a car that is perfectly well known among Porsche enthusiasts, but that nevertheless remains slightly shrouded in the mists of history. It is familiar, but at the same time unknown – and who has ever really seen one of these precursors to the legend in pictures or in real life?

That was another reason for taking a closer look at the 901 – we want to show it in detail; to be amazed by the original form that, through its simple sophistication, became one of the century's most definitive; a form that still looks as good today as it did on day one – even 50 years on. It goes without saying that this book traces the path to the 901/911 – but not in the depth of those definitive works out there. Greater emphasis was placed on talking to as many of those men as possible who actually worked on it and brought it to fruition; men who can still attest to all those trials and tribulations endured by the team until the car finally made it to the 1963 Frankfurt Motor Show – and one year later had swapped the name 901 for 911, a series of digits that has been recognized around the world ever since as the definitive symbol of the sports car genre.

A FORM THAT, EVEN 50 YEARS AFTER IT WAS CREATED, STILL LOOKS AS FRESH AS IT DID ON DAY 1.

A PROUD MAN – A PROUD CAR: FERRY PORSCHE HAS FINALLY MADE IT! IT IS 1964 AND THE 901 IS READY.

A 901 IS A 911:
THIS IS THE FORM THAT
BECAME A DESIGN ICON –
INSTANTLY RECOGNIZABLE.

SLEEK, SIMPLE, PRECISE —
THE COMPELLING EXTERIOR DESIGN
OF THE 901 TRANSLATES TO
THE INTERIOR, TOO.

IN ITS ORIGINAL FORM, THE 901 IS
A MASTER OF MINIMALISM —
NEITHER FLARED FENDERS NOR
SPOILERS DISRUPT THE LINES.

ON THE EDGE OF PERFECTION:
THE 901 IS PURE PORSCHE.

INTERIOR VENTILATION CAN BE

SO SIMPLE ...

WHERE DID WE COME FROM AND WHERE ARE WE GOING?

THE 356 FOUNDS AN EMPIRE

Porsche is a phenomenon, a paradox. Conceived and constructed from a robust people's car, the sporty variant of the Beetle emerged under the simple 356 name-plate as every man's dream on four wheels, bar none. Who could ever have imagined, shortly after the end of a devastating war, the importance that this sports car would

BUILT BY THE SWISS FOR THE SWISS: THE FIRST PORSCHE 356 CABRIOLET.

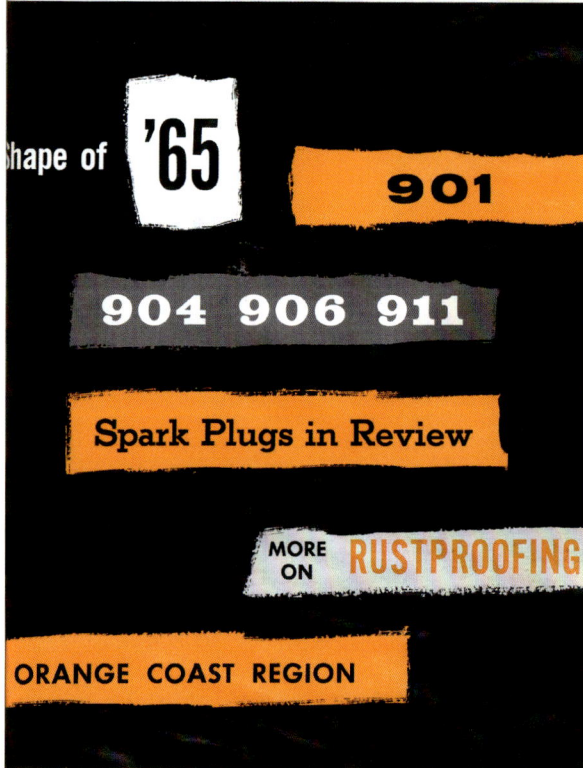

PORSCHE
PANORAMA · DECEMBER 1964

Shape of '65 901
904 906 911
Spark Plugs in Review
MORE ON RUSTPROOFING
ORANGE COAST REGION

attain in such a short period of time – as a symbol of reconstruction, as a symbol of the significance of German ingenuity, as a symbol of reliability, as a symbol of sustainability.

This importance intensified as the concept was perfected over time, and as it rapidly began to notch up successes on the world's race tracks – turning Dr. Ing. h.c. F. Porsche KG in the space of just ten years into a global symbol of sporting prowess and of German quality and reliability. It is no wonder that the Porsche 356 has enjoyed such high acclaim ever since, and to this day, from all and sundry – it was obviously a very special vehicle that (despite its high price tag) had virtually no competitors. A Porsche was simply a Porsche – and that was why so many men and women just had to own one, although there were plenty more sensible and practical vehicles around.

But, with the 356, Porsche created far more than »just« a sports car – the small Beetle derivative became the pride of a country that, back then, still did not have a whole lot of self-confidence. It also created jobs and put a great deal of money into government coffers – it was not without good reason that Ferry Porsche later said that he »always had to be so very thrifty, because the Treasury wanted its taxes on a regular basis.«

As a result of diligence, plenty of creativity, skilled craftsmen and dedicated employees, the company was able to report some extremely healthy figures as the 356 approached the end of its lifecycle – figures that nobody could possibly have imagined when the tiny »Porsche-Konstruktionen-Ges. m. b. H.« was founded in Gmünd, Austria in early 1948. The final production numbers for the Porsche 356 read as follows: Of the original 356, a total of 7627 units were built, followed by 21045 of the 356 A. The most successful version was the 356 B, which tallied an impressive 30963 units. The subsequent 356 C, considered by experts as the

DESPITE ITS HIGH PRICE, THIS CAR HAD NO COMPETITORS

CONFUSION LED TO BOTH NAMES BEING MENTIONED: 901 AND 911.

best 356, added a further 16 668 vehicles to the total – with the 911 already snapping at its heels. And it all started with two Swiss men, Rupprecht von Senger and Bernhard Blank, who were prepared to take the risk of ordering and financing the construction of 50 units in Gmünd.

There was no doubt about it – at the dawn of the 1960s, around 15 years after the company began building cars, Porsche had been able to capture a remarkable share of the exclusive sports car market. It was an unbelievable rise that was the outcome of several factors. The first was that, from 1948 on, Ferry Porsche relied on the proven underpinnings provided by the robust Beetle technology. The second was that he and his team had systematically developed and improved on the 356 and thus slowly but surely distanced his product from its somewhat mundane Beetle basis, transforming it into a distinctive vehicle in its own right. Over the years, Porsche produced an increasing number of parts itself and thus gradually also decreased its dependence on the unavoidably more sluggish development cycle of the mass-produced Beetle. When the 356 C was launched, it shared virtually no more parts with the Beetle. Yet, on the other hand, it still had so much technical commonality – rear-mounted, four-cylinder boxer engine, air cooling, torsion-bar suspension – that a certain relationship with the ubiquitous son of Wolfsburg did no harm at all.

Eventually, however, the first grumbles started to emerge that the 356 was getting a little long in the tooth, that it was nearing its limits and that the competition was not exactly dozing on the sidelines. After all, the design had ten years under its belt, and it was clear to all involved that the four-cylinder had reached the end of its useful life in terms of displacement. It was about time to start thinking about a successor.

But what kind of car should it be?

These days, you would say: Which is the best market segment for the new model? How should it be positioned? Then you would commission a market analysis – with a brief to take into account the competition, to examine the economic development of core and thriving markets. This would be detailed in a lengthy report that would then, accompanied by Marketing, be proposed and presented to the Management and Supervisory Boards in a series of extensive and elaborately compiled papers. On the back of protracted discussions, a solution would then struggle its way blinking into the light of day, where it would be subject to commentary of varying enthusiasm by analysts, then released into the world accompanied by an enormous advertising campaign and a sophisticated press event for thousands of journalists.

And to ensure that the media is perfectly prepared for this grand entrance, there would be a trickle of information up front – a sketch of the model here, or an engine workshop there; perhaps an exclusive preview for editors-in-chief or a design workshop for lifestyle media.

If you contrast that with the evolution of the Porsche 901 – which then rose to global stardom as the 911 – and take a closer look at the way the car was launched, you can see just how much the world has changed. There were one or two photos of a slightly disguised vehicle, issued discreetly as prototype images, and two or three trade publications were allowed to get a little closer to this new object of desire around the time the car was completed. And then there was the world premiere at the Frankfurt Motor Show – and that was pretty much it. As series production did not actually begin until sometime later, Porsche in-house magazine *Christophorus* set out to satisfy interest with two articles on the new flagship – while, in parallel, continuing to describe the merits of the 356 in great detail; after all, it was still on sale.

What a modest entrance – but much more than that was neither possible nor affordable. Ferry Porsche knew very well how tight the money was. And he also knew that the new model would have to be a success, or else the young company would slide headlong into bankruptcy.

WHAT A MODEST ENTRANCE – BUT THERE WAS NO MONEY FOR ADVERTISING AND EXPENSIVE PRESENTATIONS.

IT WAS GOING TO BE A *LONG* JOUR-NEY

BECAUSE OPINION ON THE *NEW* MO-DEL WAS EXTREMELY DIVIDED

Obviously, Porsche had repeatedly considered a successor, alternatives to the 356, and spent time working on concepts, design and technology. But the path to the Porsche 911 would be a long one, culminating at the Frankfurt Motor Show in September 1963 with the world premiere of the 901.

PORSCHE'S FIRST APPEARANCE WAS AT THE 1949 GENEVA MOTOR SHOW WITH THE 356/2 COUPÉ (GMÜND). IN THIS PHOTO (R. TO L.): ERNST SCHOCH (PRIVATE SECRETARY TO BERNHARD BLANK), LOUISE PIËCH, BERNHARD BLANK, FERRY PORSCHE.

on new concepts. And even as they are being created, it remains unclear whether they will ever see the light of day. These are enormously expensive sandbox games on which the rise and fall of an entire company can depend – especially if the company in question happens to be as small as Porsche was at the time and, in fact, remained until its ultimate takeover by the VW Group.

A FOUR-SEATER WAS CONSIDERED AS FAR BACK AS THE 1950s.

In the early 1950s, Ferry Porsche and his team in Zuffenhausen began to consider whether the 356 should be accompanied by a four-seater variant – at the very beginning of its production life, some customers expressed the desire for more space for the whole family and its luggage. And, inevitably, this question also led to the notion that this space problem could be solved with a further, larger model. But the 356 was still at the very start of its career and production volumes were very low. Nevertheless, Erwin Komenda – who came to Ferdinand Porsche in 1931 and had been responsible for all bodyshell design ever since – built a four-seater Porsche back in 1951 under the project number 530. In order to make room for four seats, the wheelbase was extended from 210 centimeters to 240 centimeters, while both doors were widened for easier access to the rear seats. The outcome was hardly convincing: The proportions were knocked somewhat off-beam by the longer wheelbase, and the higher curb weight put a damper on performance. Overall, it was not a great design, and only two prototypes of the Type 530 were ever built.

THE TYPE 530: NOT A GREAT DESIGN

That this model would morph into this spectacular success that remains in the lineup to this day as an indestructible evergreen was well beyond the scope of anyone's imagination back in the 1960s.

Automakers are consistently stretched between two poles – on the one side are the models of their lineup that have to be produced and sold in order to sustain the company, pay employees and secure development costs for the successor. At the other extreme, it takes around three to four years to develop a completely new model and prepare it for production. And thus the existing product lineup, and of course its buyers, is carefully nurtured, while work continues simultaneously in hermetically sealed development centers

It was during this period that two further types also made an appearance. However, to date, they have featured very little – if at all – in the Porsche history books. One was the Type 656, which was previously known only as a straightforward development of the 356. A large number of highly detailed drawings of this were generated in 1954, showing that the idea of the 530 – likewise with a wheelbase of 2400 millimeters – had indeed been re-executed with greater elegance. In summer 2010, Porsche archivist Jen Torner found a few previously lost drawings of this project that patently demonstrate the extra space on the rear seats. A passage from Ferry Porsche's biography also makes it clear that the idea of a four-seater had been tabled and considered at an early stage. »It was for this reason that we considered several variants of the 356 as a four-seater. We built a sedan, a cabriolet, a coupe – they were all sensible propositions. The cabriolet, for instance, was just 100 kilograms heavier than the 356. That was quite acceptable. The coupe, too, was

PORSCHE BUILT ITS FIRST FOUR-SEATER PROTOTYPE, THE TYPE 530, IN 1951. HOWEVER, SERIES PRODUCTION WAS NEVER SERIOUSLY CONSIDERED.

PAGE027

1600   1700   1800   1900   2000   2100   2200

F.
E.
K

K. S.

extremely interesting. But then I decided, ›enough of this, let's make a proper successor with a new engine, a six-cylinder, because the new car has to be better than the old one!‹« This secured the place of the type 656 as a further stepping stone in the 356 succession story – although nothing was ultimately to come of it.

WITH A WHEELBASE OF 2400 MM, THE TYPE 656 WAS IN-
TENDED TO PROVIDE SPACE FOR TWO LARGE REAR SEATS.

5

MR

M-H-A

2300   2400   2500   2600

FROM THE FRONT AND REAR VIEWS, THE TYPE 530 IS VIRTUALLY INDISCERNIBLE FROM A SERIES-PRODUCTION 356.

FROM THE SIDE, IT IS EVIDENT THAT THE TYPE 530 WITH FOUR SEATS WAS SOMEWHAT LACKING IN ELEGANCE.

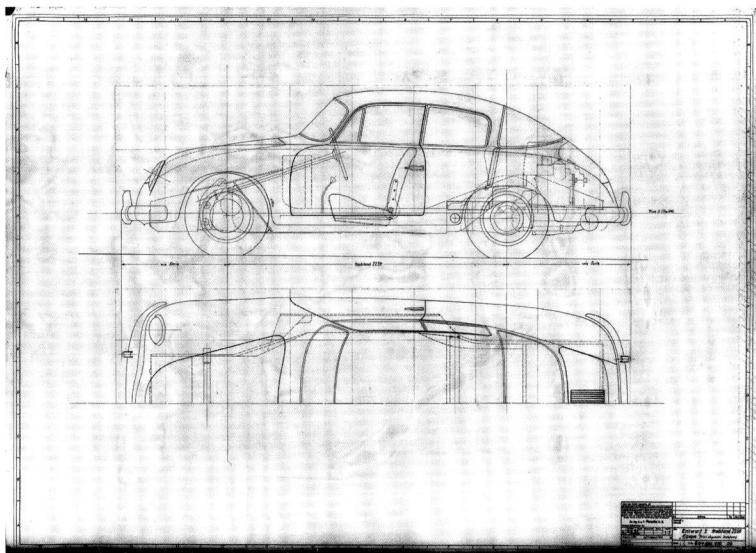

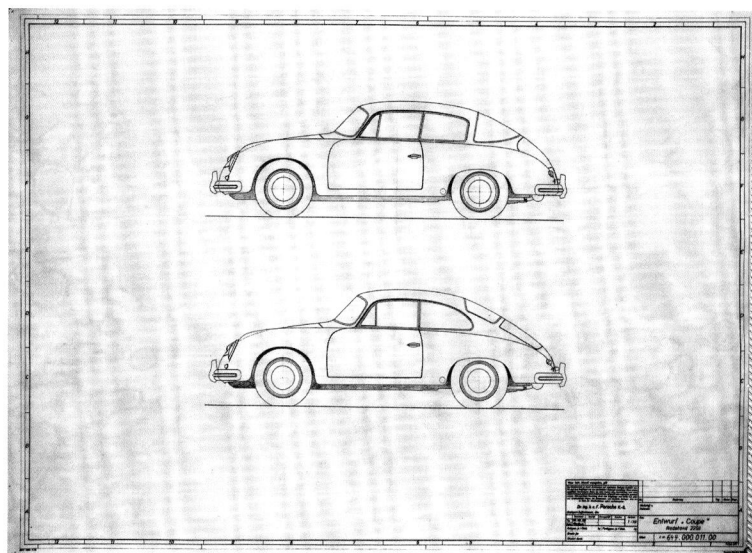

What is interesting, however, is the vehemence with which Ferry Porsche, in his many interviews with his biographer Günther Molter, defends the view that the decision on the 356 successor was taken so quickly and so clearly. The search for the »right successor« was evidently a significantly slower and more complex affair than his recollections would indicate.

After the 656 failed to lead to any kind of lasting outcome, a slew of drawings emerged just three years later bearing the designation 644 – this time with a wheelbase of 2250 millimeters. They offer some insight into how intensively Porsche had worked on the issue of increased interior space. There was Version I with a »non-offset roof shape« and Version II, a hardtop coupe – both drawings were completed on August 6, 1957. One month later came a »coupe with offset roof shape and 150 percent extended luggage space« (September 10, 1957), while a drawing from October 10 shows a coupe with the familiar roof shape alongside a coupe with a non-offset roof shape – although, it is immediately evident which design is the more elegant.

What is confusing about these drawings is the model designation, because, in summer 1957, Porsche also allocated the number 644 to a new

transmission. Karl Ludvigsen wrote about this as follows: »The new transmission was initially introduced in line with availability, first in the Speedster, then also gradually in the other models. The new transmission with its own 644 part reference was a departure from the two-part magnesium casting carried over from VW, being made instead from a one-piece aluminum casting. Because the transmission's gears and shafts were fitted from one end into the casing's tunnel-like cavity, the 644 quickly earned the nickname ›tunnel-casing‹ gearbox. Thus it would appear that Porsche had – as it often did – given the same designation to two projects. This was apparently also true for the predecessor to the 901, known by the reference 695, which also appeared for the first time in drawings and sketches around this time. In this case, the numerical reference had actually been allocated to new disc brakes that were scheduled for development.«

THE TYPE 644 REAPPEARED ON AUGUST 6, 1957 – HERE WITH A WHEELBASE OF 2250 MILLIMETERS (L.).
THE DRAWING OF A 644 COUPÉ WAS COMPLETED ON OCTOBER 10 – BENEATH IT THE SIDE VIEW OF A 356 (R.).

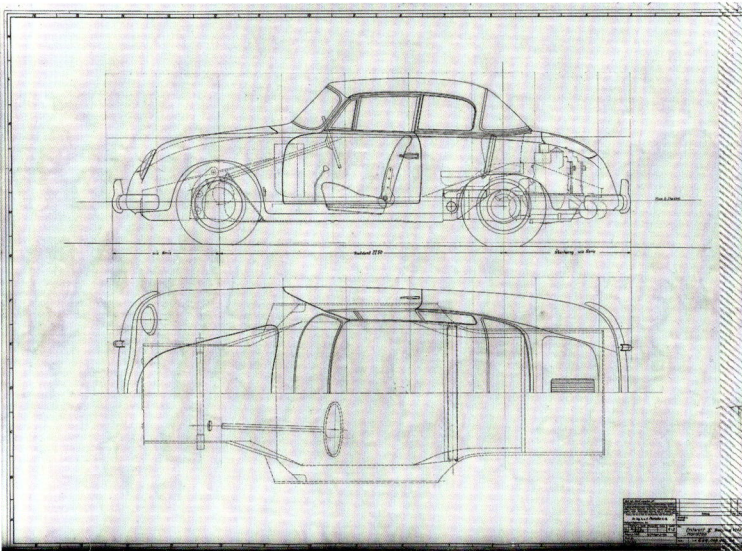

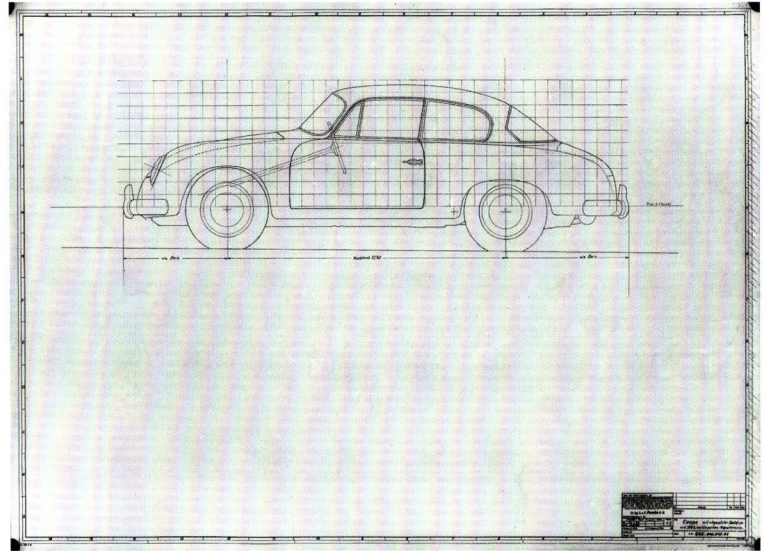

But in 1957 there was still no definitive direction – and Ferry Porsche's team was still on the receiving end of requests from customers and sales force alike for a more family-friendly 356 – which can hardly make it surprising that the issue of a four-seater repeatedly reared its head over the next few years. And because the sales team continually raised the subject of more space, there also existed a loose relationship with a few independent coachbuilders. One in particular was Swiss coachbuilder Beutler.

The company founded in 1946 already had experience with this kind of bodyshell reconstruction – because this is where, between January and August 1949, the first six Porsche 356/2 Cabriolets were created. Ernst Beutler recalled in 1997: »The cooperation in 1948/49 with Professor Ferdinand Porsche senior was a very special experience. He was convincing, certain and uncomplicated. Following the great success – 6 cabriolets – further production

in Thun was impossible. Porsche then moved from Gmünd to Stuttgart and began its cooperation with coachbuilder Reutter.« Some time later came the cooperation with the VW factory – at the 1954 Geneva Motor Show, the Swiss company from Thun had unveiled a sports car based on the Beetle as a 2+2-seater coupe and cabriolet. The Beutler sports coupes and cabriolets, which were made from sheet aluminum, were among the most expensive special bodies on the Beetle chassis at the time – pricing started at 15950 Swiss Francs. A total of 19 of them were ultimately built in Thun's Gwattstraße – much sought-after rarities these days.

That Porsche was unable to free itself from the four-seater issue became evident once more in fall 1958, when Ferry Porsche contracted Fritz Beutler and his younger brother Ernst to build a larger version of the 356 A. To this end, a 356 A chassis was sent from Reutter to Thun, where Beutler extended it by 250 millimeters and then, in winter 1958/59, built a new bodyshell. With VW and Porsche well aware of the quality of the Swiss bodyshell specialists,

LIKE SO MANY OTHER DESIGNS, THE TYPE 644 FAILED TO MAKE IT OFF THE DRAWING BOARD – THE 356 WAS STILL TOO STRONG.

THE EARLIEST DRAWING OF A TYPE 644 DATES BACK TO FEBRUARY 6, 1957 AND SHOWS A HARDTOP DESIGN (L.).
644 »COUPÉ WITH OFFSET ROOF SHAPE AND 150% EXTENDED LUGGAGE COMPARTMENT« – DRAWN ON SEPTEMBER 10, 1957 (R.).

AVAILABLE
FOR
IMMEDIATE
DELIVERY

S. Thompson Tjaarda
Via Pomba 23
Torino, Italia

Dr. Ing. h.c.F. Porsche K. G.
Stuttgart, Zuffenhausen
Porsch Strasse, Germany

Dear Sirs;
    Being an architect as well as a Porsche
owner, I have no small interest as to the future
of your automobile. The designs which I have
sent and which you have probably studied by now
have been seen by no one except you and a friend
of mine who encouraged me to send them to you.
    I sent the original drawings instead of
prints or photographs in hoping that you will have
more confidence in me. I have one print of the
design which I kept myself. Since I am a consultant I have no studio large enough to develope
scale models, so would like to make the following
proposition if you are interested. It is
obvious that you could use these drawings without
anyone knowing the difference, however, it is
for your interest alone that I say that it is
better to let the original designer develope the
shape of the automobile to its best proportions.
    Therefore, if arrangements could be made with
you, I could come directly to your establishment
to work with your designers for two or three weeks.
However, the only time I could do this is between
the 6th. and the 26th. of August since I am taking
this as my vacation period. The cost would be what
you think right plus your daily consultant expence
allounce. I am anxious to hear your answer since
time is getting short before I leave for my vacation.

    Sincerely
    S. Thompson Tjaarda

S. THOMPSON TJAARDA WAS CLEARLY VERY SURE OF HIMSELF — HE WANTED TO DESIGN THE NEXT PORSCHE GENERATION IN
TWO TO THREE WEEKS. HIS TIME WAS INDEED LIMITED, BY SEPTEMBER I HE WAS UNDER CONTRACT WITH PININFARINA.

Beutler was very intimately involved with the project. However, it never led to the closer cooperation for which Porsche had been hoping because the relatively angular »full-view coupé« did not meet with great enthusiasm from the designers in Zuffenhausen. Added to that, the Beutler brothers were not particularly keen to embark on a significant enlargement of their small but fine company for a somewhat difficult piece of business, especially as it would involve substantial financial investment. Ernst Beutler once more, »Then a further cooperation with Porsche came in 1958. Our project to build a four-seat coupé based on the 356 S 90 chassis met with approval. The undercarriage was extended by 250 millimeters in our workshop. The tooling and production jig was made in cooperation with Porsche engineers. It was very successful, but the production numbers for us were very low because the Porsche 911 appeared with more room in the back.« In total, seven vehicles of this type were produced. After the first vehicle, which is now part of a collection in Germany, a cabriolet was built to order for Count von Württemberg in May 1959. These were followed between November 1959 and November 1961 by five more coupés – now based on the 356 B with a wheelbase extended by 200 millimeters – all of which were exported to the USA. These five coupés, which were visually far closer to the 356, had a more rounded form that was considerably more elegant and embodied the very essence of Swiss understatement.

The level of interest in the Porsche topic on the part of designers is also apparent in another letter that Stevens Thompson Tjaarda sent to Porsche in July 1961 together with a drawing. Tjaarda had worked from 1958 until 1960 at Carrozzeria Ghia in Turin, followed by a few months at Gabetti & Isola (architects and furniture designers) before moving to Pininfarina in September 1961. However, the letter to Porsche was written at the time when Tjaarda still was considering a return to car design – and he immediately offered himself as consultant and designer for the next Porsche models with the following words:

Dear Sirs;

Being an architect as well as a Porsche owner, I have no small interest as to the future of your automobile. The designs which I have sent and which you have probably studied by now have been seen by no one except you and a friend of mine who encouraged me to send them to you.

I sent the original drawings instead of prints or photographs in hoping that you will have more confidence in me. I have one print of the design which I kept myself. Since I am a consultant I have no studio large enough to develope [sic] scale models, so would like to make the following proposition if you are interested. It is obvious that you could use these drawings without anyone knowing the difference, however, it is for your interest alone that I say that it is better to let the original designer develop the shape of the automobile to its best proportions.

Therefore, if arrangements could be made with you, I could come directly to your establishment to work with your designers for two or three weeks. However, the only time I could do this is between the 6th and the 26th of August since I am taking this as my vacation period. The cost would be what you think right plus your daily consultant expense allounce [sic]. I am anxious to hear your answer since time is getting short before I leave for my vacation.

Sincerely
S. Thompson Tjaarda

That was certainly a self-confident letter that Tom Tjaarda sent to Porsche just a few days after his 27th birthday. He later went on to design a few famous Ferrari models when he was with Pininfarina, as well as the De Tomaso Pantera while working for Ghia and Ford. Whether his letter to Porsche ever received an answer is now lost in the mists of time.

And in 1962, even Carrozzeria Ghia itself ventured a proposal for a four-seat and four-door 356, for which the Italians extended the wheelbase by no less than 35 centimeters – something that did not do much for the aesthetics.

I AM ANXIOUS TO HEAR YOUR ANSWER SINCE TIME IS GETTING SHORT …

But back to 1957: While the Beutler brothers were still contemplating the market chances of a four-seat coupe, those at Porsche decided to take another serious look at the issue in Zuffenhausen. On one side, the in-house design department was set the task of developing a four-seat variant, while Albrecht Graf Goertz was commissioned to do the same, having just created a memorial to himself and the Bayerische Motorenwerke with the BMW 507.

Albrecht Graf Goertz wrote in his memoirs on the topic, »BMW was a very different company to the one it is today. Meals were served in the board members' dining room on a long table, to which Dr. Ferry Porsche was also invited as a guest one day. Porsche congratulated me on the BMW 507 and requested that I drop in to see him on my next visit to Stuttgart. So, after my six-month anti-competition clause with BMW had expired, I drove to Stuttgart to meet with Dr. Porsche. We spoke about the possibilities of developing a full-grown four-seater that would replace the 356. And we quickly came to an agreement – which is always easier to do when you can deal directly with the boss of a company, because he does not then have to go through the laborious process of securing board approval.

AT THE BEHEST OF FERRY PORSCHE, COACHBUILDING FIRM BEUTLER ALSO MADE AN ATTEMPT AT A FOUR-SEATER – SIX VEHICLES WERE ULTIMATELY BUILT (ABOVE). ALBRECHT GRAF GOERTZ RECEIVED THE COMMISSION FROM FERRY PORSCHE TO DESIGN A FOUR-SEAT PORSCHE (BELOW).

In the course of this conversation, Dr. Porsche told me that he had a son that was studying at the School of Design in Ulm. Because I have always had my doubts about overly formal educations at design schools, which delve too much into theory, I recommended that the young man should leave the School of Design in Ulm and work together with me on this project. Ferdinand Alexander Porsche did not return to Ulm, but instead came to me in the Porsche design studio, which was located on the factory site in Zuffenhausen – that was probably the most important contribution I ever made to the future of Porsche.

I worked with the team to draw and build a 1:1 plaster model of a four-seat, two-door coupe, and we then invited Mrs. Louise Piëch – Dr. Porsche's sister – to attend a presentation of the model. The two siblings walked around the model several times, spoke with one another and then came to me and said, ›That is a very beautiful car – but it is a Goertz and not a Porsche.‹

I asked myself if I had been incorrectly instructed – but when was a briefing ever truly perfect? This model and a second design were both rejected, and that was the end of my professional cooperation with Porsche. On a personal level, we maintained friendly contact and, ultimately, the Porsche experience imparted some invaluable knowledge: It is so easy to draw a car for oneself – but far more difficult to develop a vehicle for a company like Porsche, Mercedes-Benz or BMW.«

Obviously, others involved saw and see the situation differently. Ferdinand Alexander Porsche described his view of things in an interview with Tobias Aichele thus: »Goertz stuck strictly to the brief of designing a vehicle with a larger interior and a fastback. However, it was apparent from the very

»IT IS EASY TO DESIGN A CAR FOR ONESELF – BUT DIFFICULT TO DEVELOP A VEHICLE SPECIFICALLY FOR A COMPANY.«

»THAT IS A VERY BEAUTIFUL CAR – BUT IT IS A GOERTZ AND NOT A PORSCHE«, WAS THE COMMENT MADE BY LOUISE PIËCH AND FERRY PORSCHE ON THE DESIGN PRODUCED BY ALBRECHT GRAF GOERTZ IN 1957 FOR THE ZUFFENHAUSEN COMPANY.

first sketches that the car would come over as too idiosyncratic and too American. Despite this, Ferry Porsche insisted on modeling one of the designs in the model-making department in 1:1 scale. Because the design would have to be paid for anyway, he wanted to have a model of it.«

And thus, the Goertz adventure ended – Tobias Aichele on the end of this model: »While styling elements of the later 911 are evident in the side view of the Goertz model, the front view in particular, with its twin headlamps, is far too restless and American.« Looking at the angular rear end, it was the three round lights on each side that stood out above all. In spite of this, the design was still not rejected at this point. In order to make a more realistic assessment of the three-tonne model, it would be necessary to build a version with real glass, which would be incredibly expensive to do. Two model-makers were tasked with the job of creating a negative mold made up of five parts: the two side views, the front, the rear and the roof section. Before the plaster mold could be laid with polyester, the project was stopped. Ferry Porsche, who also saw the costs running away from him, summed it up as »a beautiful Goertz,

WE
EXISTED
IN A
WONDERFUL
NICHE

ALBRECHT GRAF GOERTZ DREW ANOTHER MODEL BASED ON THE TYPE 695, AND DUBBED IT »JUNIOR«.

but not a Porsche.« The plaster molds were destroyed two years later.

This quickly brought to an end the dream of having a new Porsche designed by a great name from outside the company – from this point on, the in-house design department created the forms that would characterize the brand for decades to come.

In parallel, however, Ferry Porsche had also commissioned a second variant that combined two models in one. The one half was – as already indicated by Graf Goertz – designed by him, the other half was created by the Porsche model-making department under the management of Heinrich Klie, who was acting Head of Design at the time. This model, too, emerged as an interesting development, because the front ends of both designs were remarkably similar with their highly curved fenders – although Goertz was unable to resist the temptation of introducing a little glamour with indicator lamps set into the substantial bumper, while Klie's headlamps, recessed into the fender and smoothed with aerodynamic cladding, were a particularly elegant detail. Another interesting feature is the pleat in the front lid, which gave the front end a greater degree of tension – and would later find its way in a similar form into series production. There were clear differences, however, in the rear ends, whereby Heinrich Klie stuck more to the typical Porsche design language, while Goertz took the fastback theme seriously, giving the rear a large, extended window that had a massive visual impact on this part of the model. And here, too, Goertz opted for high, large and heavy bumpers, which – most likely chromed in series-production – would have detracted a great deal from the lightness and elegance of a typical Porsche.

However, this model was also important because it marked the first appearance of the 695 designation – as evidenced by the associated drawing from May 17, 1957. It is also interesting that on the drawing bearing the reference 695.500.101.00 only the Klie variant is visible; the second half by Goertz is missing. Whether that was intentional – or the other drawings have simply disappeared over the last half century – is unclear. It is surprising, though, that the number 695 was then allocated again around two years later to the new disc brakes for the 901 project.

It is interesting that the Klie »half« was immortalized two years later with a few details in the prototype with the designation T7. However, it has to be said that neither of the models from Graf Goertz and Heinrich Klie had really hit the spot for Ferry Porsche at the time. He still had something else in mind – and the idea of a four-seat coupe was still not entirely off the table after this particular experience, but it was certainly put on the back burner. It became increasingly apparent that the boss neither wanted nor could enter into competition with other sedan manufacturers. He is reported as later recalling, »We existed in a wonderful niche. With a sedan, we would have had to go up against the biggest in the industry – and we would probably have lost.«

It must also be said that the automotive industry at the time had a completely different structure from the one that exists today. Each manufacturer still represented specific segments – Mercedes-Benz stood for large sedans and exceptional sports cars like the 300 SL; there was Borgward with its sporty sedans, and BMW still did not really know if it should go with the big six and eight-cylinders or stick with the Isetta. Opel and Ford were mass producers obviously managed by their American parent companies and standing for cost-effective, reliable, volume models, while Volkswagen stood for mass mobility. In this clearly structured model portfolio, Porsche was a sporty outsider that got in nobody's way – the few Mercedes 300 SL and BMW 507 models played in another league, while the 190 SL was more of a vehicle for the ladies. Otherwise, sports cars came from Italy and Great Britain – brands like Alfa Romeo, Triumph and MG were well represented, and the few rich people out there dreamt of Ferrari, Maserati and Aston Martin. Nobody had yet seen a Corvette, never mind driven one.

It is no wonder, then, that Ferry Porsche felt very little inclination to take a big risk with a four-seater. Ultimately, it would have been considered among the natural rivals to Mercedes-Benz, and that was already too big a name for the young company from Zuffenhausen, which did not really want to enter into that kind of competition – Ferry Porsche did not have the time for that,

THE FRONT END OF THE LATER 901 IS ALREADY EVIDENT — THIS MODEL WAS DESIGNED HALF AND HALF
BY GRAF GOERTZ (THE RIGHT-HAND SIDE) AND HEINRICH KLIE (THE LEFT-HAND SIDE).

and he certainly did not perceive his company in that context. Thus, both four-seat studies were more like test pieces to probe the feasibility of a model range on a longer wheelbase.

But Goertz had left more of an impression in Zuffenhausen than he thought, because, in parallel to his work for Porsche, the company had obviously continued to work on ongoing improvements to the 356. In 1955, a new internal designation for the model ranges was added to the Porsche lexicon. With the introduction of the 1955 model year, the previously used T0 designation – where *T* stood for *Technical Program* – was replaced by the T1. As the 356 A, this represented the first major step away from the Beetle toward independent technology. In 1956, the T1 became the T2, which included the first introduction of the hardtop for the cabriolet, and the parallel program for the further development of the T3 was rejected again, which is why there was never a T3 variant of the 356.

What is interesting in this context, however, is Technical Program 4 – or T4 – which, from fall 1958, was intended to fulfill all sorts of things on the wish list of engineers and sales personnel alike. These included a new dashboard, pivoting sunshades and a more attractive steering wheel. This coincided with the deletion of the less powerful, 1.3-liter engine; a new Porsche should now start with at least 75 hp. Just as important was also a considerable rework of the styling – giving rise for the first and only time to a 356 front end with those American double headlamps that Goertz had just presented in his model around the same time. Although contemporary witnesses insist that this variant was never seriously considered, a detailed 1:1 clay model was nevertheless produced. It reproduced in great detail the notion of four headlamps, complete with a lifted bumper arrangement and different indicator layout options on the left and right. But if you are completely honest, you have to admit that the T4

does not really possess that hallmark Porsche elegance. It was an intellectual exercise that was never intended for realization, but brought instead to series-production maturity as the T5 – or 356 B.

But time was of the essence – and Ferry Porsche was convinced more than ever that it would soon be necessary to start thinking seriously about a successor, as the 356 would ultimately reach the end of its development potential in the not all too distant future. A displacement of more than 2 liters was definitely not feasible. And while the Carrera top model had a very sporty and powerful engine with four camshafts, this power unit was not only very expensive to produce, it was also extremely difficult to maintain – only absolute experts were able to keep it alive. The engine was originally designed by Ernst Fuhrmann to meet demands from sporty drivers for a fittingly adequate power plant, but it was utterly unsuitable for production in larger volumes. It was therefore time to start a new chapter in the Porsche story.

IN 1958, THE PORSCHE T4 PROJECT CONSIDERED THE NOTION OF FOUR HEADLAMPS AND A HIGHER BUMPER ARRANGEMENT.

THE *SUCCESSOR* IS WITHIN REACH

BUT IT LEADS TO *DIVISION*

1957 and 1958 were spent on the initial designs created by Albrecht Graf Goertz and Heinrich Klie in order to settle the issue of how things could proceed with the vehicles from Zuffenhausen – Ferry Porsche and his sister came to the realization that they did not want to take the

GRAND PRIX RACING COST PORSCHE A GREAT DEAL OF MONEY – THE 804 PICTURED IN MONZA IN 1962.

recommended routes. Nevertheless, it took some time before Ferry Porsche approved a design and development program for the successor, and for the project to finally get underway, initially under the 695 designation. The reason was the tremendously high load exerted on the small number of engineers at the time – Porsche was still a very small company.

On the one hand, refinements had to continue on the 356 – it was, after all, the model that earned the money needed for wages and salaries, as well as for the development of the type 695 and its associated driveline. On the other hand, there was also plenty of external consultancy work to do. Although it brought money into the coffers, it also took up technical capacity. In parallel to the ruminations on the 356 successor, this period also saw further development work carried out on Porsche tractors – and engineering consultancy services obviously also remained available to the likes of Volkswagen and other companies.

In addition to all this, technical and financial involvement in race cars was also on the increase – the 356 Carrera and the various mid-engine Spyders were cleaning up virtually every race and title of the time. When the CSI – the »Commission Sportive International«, the highest governing body for motorsport regulations – announced in October 1958 that Formula 1 would be restricted to a maximum engine displacement of 1.5 liters as of 1961, Porsche also began to consider intensifying its involvement in Formula racing. Of course, this development resulted not only in the first 718 RSK race cars with a mid-seat, mid-steering setup, not to mention several impressive victories, it also led to the cost-intensive construction of thoroughbred single-seaters. The years that followed brought with them the design and build of a 1.5-liter eight-cylinder for Formula 1. Although it achieved victory at the French Grand Prix in 1962 in the hands of Dan Gurney, it ultimately cost so much money and engineering capacity that the program was cancelled at the end of 1962.

No wonder that German magazine *Der Spiegel* wrote in a title story about Porsche on October 4, 1961: »The blossoming production of fast sports cars, however, is just the outward representation of the company's significance. The truth of Porsche's special position within the automotive industry is apparent through neither its production figures nor its sporting success: It is based on the hidden activities of an engineering elite in the design offices and test cells of the Zuffenhausen factory. The company runs a secret miracle works for technical development that – in contrast to the design and testing departments of other car factories – takes on contracts from other companies,

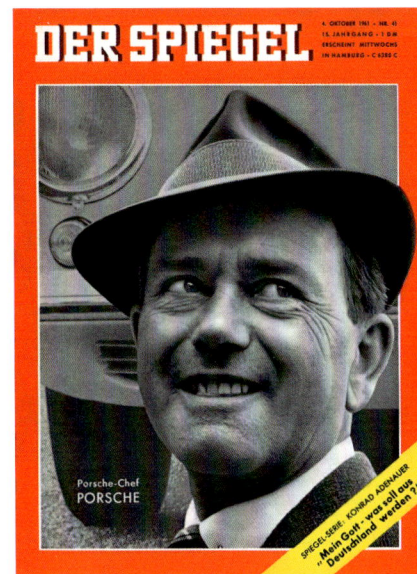

GP SPORT QUICKLY BECAME TOO EXPENSIVE

even bitter rivals, and executes them with a widely acknowledged resourcefulness. An apparently never-ending stream of consultancy fees and license income provides some indication of the high esteem in which Porsche is held in this field by its corporate customers. The very specific nature of this operation also explains the unusual composition of the workforce, which, at the end of 1960, consisted of 732 hourly-paid workers and no less than 518 salaried staff. Porsche employs far more engineers and draftsmen than a factory of this size actually needs for its own requirements, because 50 percent of the capacity of the Porsche design function is constantly occupied on third-party contract work.

Third-party clients come to Porsche with their development wishes primarily because it has several talented specialists in virtually every automotive engineering discipline. Porsche is therefore able to deliver usable

FERRY PORSCHE WITH KARL RABE IN THE WORKS I DESIGN OFFICE IN 1957.

IN OCTOBER 1961 *DER SPIEGEL* MAGAZINE TOOK A GREAT INTEREST IN PORSCHE AND ITS BUSINESS MODEL.

DURING THIS TIME, PORSCHE ALSO EARNED GOOD MONEY WITH TRACTORS (ABOVE).
PORSCHE ACQUIRED THE SITE FOR ITS DEVELOPMENT CENTER FROM THE COMMUNITY OF WEISSACH IN 1961 (BELOW).

results faster than some more narrowly skilled test departments at larger car plants.

Another reason for awarding development contracts to Zuffenhausen in particular is that Porsche employs a very specific type of engineer – the so-called driving engineer. These highly paid technicians (Ferry Porsche: ›Every one of them could be the boss elsewhere.‹) unite two rare characteristics: They have the driving habits of a grand prix driver, but are also able to use the car's handling characteristics to draw those technical conclusions enabled by the respective tests. This kind of first-class universal engineer is so rare that they simply do not exist at any other German automaker except for Porsche – and in a smaller number at Daimler-Benz and BMW.

Ferry Porsche: ›I do everything with my crew – from a complete prototype, to submitting a patent application for a simple stop for a quarter light.‹ Within the automotive industry, this role earns more than just recognition for the crew captain. ›We are not held in particularly high regard by the engineers at other factories,‹ says Ferry Porsche. ›Although, when we bring success, the sales people like us a great deal.‹ When it comes to its external contracts, Porsche often has to accept the condition that it must remain silent about its work for specific clients. The companies in question want to promote Porsche's work as having come from their own hands. As a result, the Porsche engineering department has designed a series of prototypes for a number of different third-party clients, but has to keep their technical details strictly confidential. The only certainty is that the prototypes do not always make it to series production.

One ingenious Porsche patent in particular turned out to be a resounding success. Porsche developed a new kind of synchromesh transmission (ring synchronization). It brought not only design benefits, but was also technically superior to conventional forms of synchronization – the Porsche transmission has faster shift times. It is no wonder, therefore, that English racing stable ›Vanwall‹, Italian race car builder Ferrari and even Daimler-Benz AG (for its successful Mercedes type W 196 race cars from 1954 and 1955) took advantage of the benefits of the fast-shifting transmission devised by Porsche engineer Leopold Schmid. The Porsche transmission system finds civilian applications with German companies BMW and Hans Glas GmbH, France's Simca works, Italian company Alfa Romeo and major British vehicle makers BMC and Meadows. Specialists estimate that Porsche earns a license fee of eight German Marks per truck transmission and two Marks for each passenger car transmission. Porsche also receives further substantial license fees from ›Porsche-Diesel-Motorenbau GmbH‹ in Friedrichshafen, which shares only its name with the Zuffenhausen works. It is a subsidiary of Mannesmann AG and builds agricultural tractors based on the System Porsche.

Porsche harvests third-party work in other ways, too. American giant General Motors, for example, tested its rear-engined ›Chevrolet Corvair‹ with Porsche engines in order to evaluate the experience gleaned by Porsche in rear-engine drive. Conversely, Porsche tests the products of other car manufacturers, because Porsche engineers have to derive data from third-party vehicles in their own tests conducted as part of design contracts. It says something about the variety of problems facing the Porsche engineering department that the technicians in Zuffenhausen work on the development of industrial engines (including those for agricultural uses, fire engines, generators, cranes and hoists) and even on aircraft engines derived from an automotive base unit. Porsche builds engines for an American helicopter manufacturer and for a series of hobby aircraft.

The esteem in which the ingenious inventions generated by the workers at the Zuffenhausen ideas factory are held is evident not only on the basis of fee income. Ferry Porsche: ›Everybody steals; virtually nothing can be protected.‹ Porsche's engineers see the imitation of their ideas as a benchmark for the quality of their work. A wry joke circulating within the company says, ›If something is not stolen within at least a year, then it wasn't good.‹«

DER SPIEGEL: »PORSCHE IS ABLE TO DELIVER FASTER RESULTS THAN SOME TEST DEPARTMENTS AT LARGER PLANTS.«

Vorschläge f. Typ 695

Versuch	Verkauf	H. v. Rücker	H. Porsche
Karosserie im allgemein:			
—	Bisherige Porschelinie beibehalten. Kein grundsätzlich neuer Wagen. Sportl. Charakter.		
Sitz anzahl.			
2-Sitzer mit 2 bequemen Notsitzen	2-Sitzer m. 2 bequemen Notsitzen. Notsitze f. Nebenverkehr ohne groß. Gepäck.		2-Sitzer mit 2 beqm. Notsitzen
Gepäckraum	bei 4 Pers. hint. den Rücksitzen und erweiterter Raum in der vorderen Deckel		Zunkklinke gegen → Kotflügel einbeziehen
größerer Gepäckraum über Kofferraumbeleuchtg	bei 2 Personen wesentlich größer als jetzt.		
	bessere Zugänglichkeit zum Gepäckraum.		
Einstieg			besserer Einstieg
	besserer Einstieg		
Scheiben - Sicht	bessere Rücksicht heizbare Scheibe.		vollsicht
größere Halbscheibe zum Sicht			
Scheinwerfer	besseres Scheinwerferlicht weite + Breite		Weiters an allen Strömungs Hinsicht verkleidet.
größere und tieferalt angeordnet	Parkleuchte links		
Ersatzscheinwerfer muss behelfsgd. eingebaut werden können.	bessere Blinker vorn u. hinten		
Blink u. Bremsleuchten größer u. günstiger anordnen nicht mehrere Funktionen in einer Leuchte.			
Stoßstangen			
bessere Stoßstangen	bessere Stoßstangen in günstigerer Lage		
			Spaltflügel ausbildung f. amerik. Stoßstange interess.

WE LEARNT A GREAT DEAL VERY QUICKLY BACK THEN

After this big title story appeared in the renowned *Spiegel* it was clear to outsiders, too, that Zuffenhausen was home to not only an extraordinarily prolific, but also a qualitatively first-class team; a team that sometimes – as those involved at the time like to concede – worked round the clock with remarkable dedication. Something the spritely seniors still look on to this day with a degree of fascination. »We worked from early in the morning until late at night,« recalls Herbert Linge, »and the matter of overtime was not a major issue either for us or the work's council.« Hans Mezger adds, »In such a small team, you also took on responsibility at a very early stage – and it was also a source of motivation when you were actually able to make things happen.« And Paul Hensler, who was Head of Development, Mechanics by the end of his service with Porsche, still asks himself to this day how, with around 30 people in testing and 30 people in engineering, it was even possible to manage a workload of that size. But, »as young employees, we really enjoyed these fascinating jobs and such a high degree of responsibility. We learnt a great deal very quickly back then.«

However, despite all the other jobs, it was now time to start seriously addressing the issue of a successor to the 356 – a task that, in true Porsche fashion, received the designation Technical Program 7 or T7. Ferry Porsche once more described how he envisaged the T7: the 356 B + XX centimeters – although there had still been no discussions as to whether the matter of a full four-seater was now completely off the table or not. In any event, the new model had to be a typical Porsche with two seats and a somewhat larger rear bench, and have the classic Porsche fastback. This is where the issue of tradition came into play – Ferry Porsche had absolutely no intention of challenging his loyal customers with design experiments, something he had determined and decided at least by the time the Goertz model came along.

Fortunately, a search of the archive delivered a hand-written list with suggestions for the type 695 on which testing, sales and Mr. Porsche outline their opinions on the successor to the 356. Although Mr. von Rücker (Head of Technical Development) is named on the two notes, he obviously never received them as his input is missing. These pages, which were probably created in 1957 or 1958, provide the guidelines for orientation of the design and technology. The sales function demanded, »Not a fundamentally new car. Sporty character. Significantly larger for two people than at present. Better entry. Better rear view.« The engineers demanded more practical things, »Better visibility. Larger and more vertical headlamps. Better bumpers.« And Ferry Porsche made it perfectly clear, »2-seater with 2 comfortable jump seats.« These recommendations for the type 695 delivered a pretty precise definition of the concept.

Following a short time at the School of Design in Ulm, Ferdinand Alexander Porsche then joined the design offices of Porsche KG in 1957, which were under the leadership of Erwin Komenda. He then quickly began to inject new energy into Porsche Design – energy that would ultimately manifest itself in the aesthetic perfection of the 904 Carrera GTS and the 901/911. Ferdinand Alexander (F. A.) Porsche and his small team started this work with initial sketches of a 356 chassis extended by 30 centimeters. It was a rather remarkable wheelbase that was strictly speaking too long to meet the clear instructions issued by Ferry Porsche for a »2-seater with 2 comfortable jump seats«. But the somewhat changeable history of prototypes was never particularly stringent. This phase casts up yet another problem with historical representation, as the final result of all ruminations and developments over the years that followed, which would then become known as T7, appears in the memories

THE CONCEPT FOR THE 356 SUCCESSOR WAS DEFINED BY RECOMMENDATIONS MADE FOR THE TYPE 695.

of those involved – and in all literature associated with the development of the 901 – under two different model designations. It is known both as the type 695 and as the type 754.

ONE CAR – AND TWO MODEL DESIGNATIONS: THE T7 BEGAN LIFE AS THE TYPE 695 AND AS THE TYPE 754.

Newly unearthed drawings now appear to shed light on this mystery. They clearly indicate that the T7 was still known as the type 695 until the end of 1960. In parallel to the various drawings and models, however, 1960 also saw work commence on the construction of the first drivable T7 – and this vehicle was afforded the type 754 designation. This could be a conclusive solution that explains why the T7 was so often and to such confusion associated with both model designations. It would appear that the 695 never attained the status of a drivable prototype – this was preserved for the type 754. And the construction of drivable and functioning type 754 probably also started in parallel with the development of the type 695 – or at least on an only slightly offset timescale, once the planning and drawing of the type 695 was already underway.

In any event, Ferdinand Alexander Porsche had set to work and, over the course of the years that followed, developed his own classic form on the basis of the 695; a form that was already closer to the ultimate design. Emerging in parallel, under the direction of Claus von Rücker, the then Head of Technical Development, was the technology for the new vehicle. Rücker, who was appointed by Ferry Porsche as a technical consultant in 1955, was afforded the title of Chief Engineer in early 1956. Prior to the war, the German had worked for BMW in its motorsport department, moving after the war via Canada to the USA, where he quickly made his mark at Studebaker, ultimately taking over the position of Deputy Head of Testing and Development. The fact that Claus von Rücker could consequently work and do business in perfect English was an additional plus during those years in which the US market was becoming increasingly important for Porsche.

Interestingly, the 695 designation was used not only for the T7 design and development program, but also for the disc brakes that the engineers developed for the 356 successor – but this kind of overlap is not unusual at Porsche. And, while Claus von Rücker and his team were having their initial thoughts on the new bodyshell, the small team led by Ferdinand Alexander »Butzi« Porsche set about their first sketches, which were rapidly followed by small

THE TEAM IN THE DESIGN STUDIO WAS A SMALL ONE: (FROM LEFT) HEINRICH KLIE, HANS PLOCH, HANS SPRINGMANN, ERNST BOLT AND FERDINAND ALEXANDER PORSCHE IN 1963.

IN THE INITIAL PHASE, THE T7
WAS STILL A TYPE 695 – HERE
WITH A WHEELBASE OF 2350
MILLIMETERS AND THE TYPE
745 ENGINE, WHICH WOULD
REMAIN A ONE-OFF.

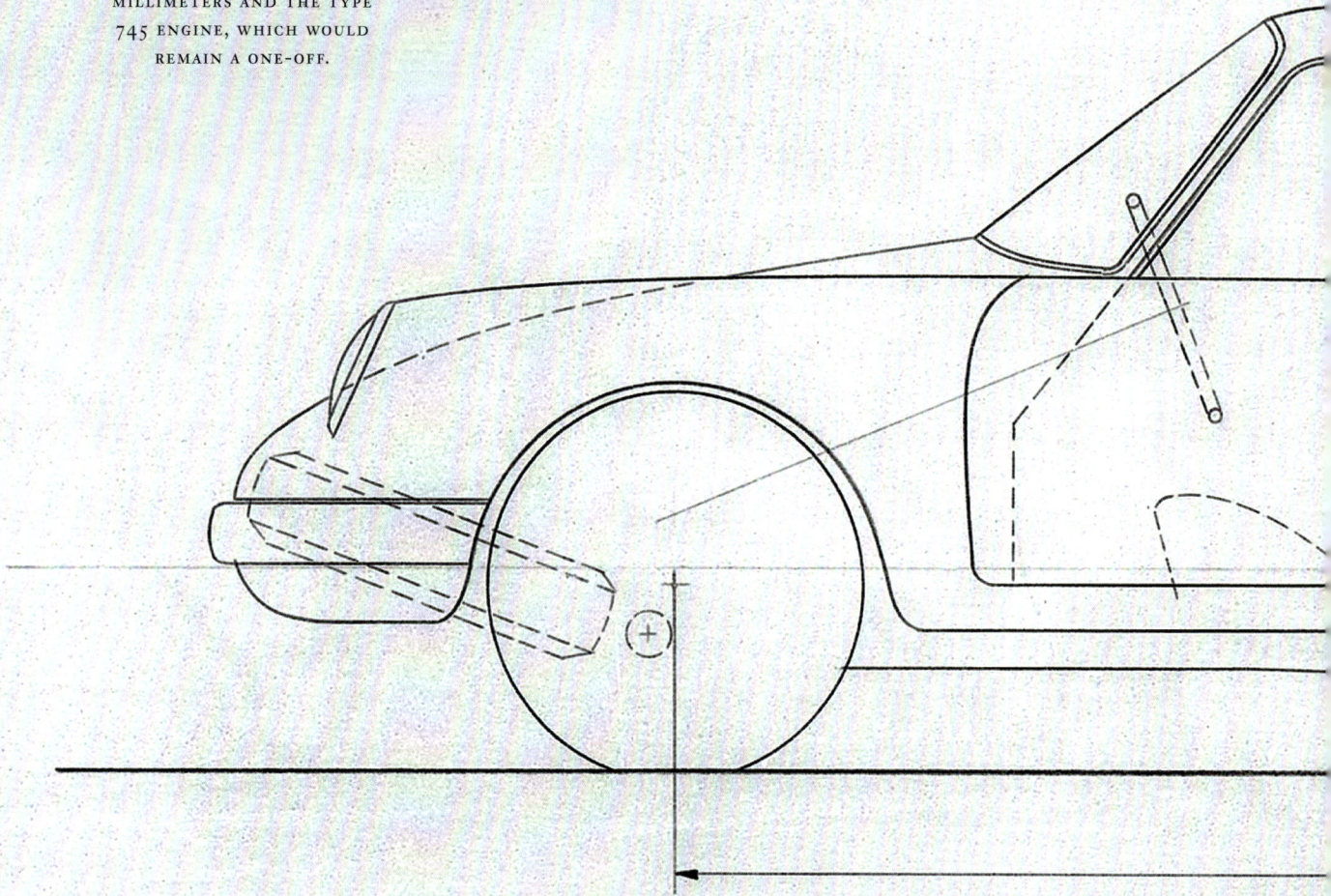

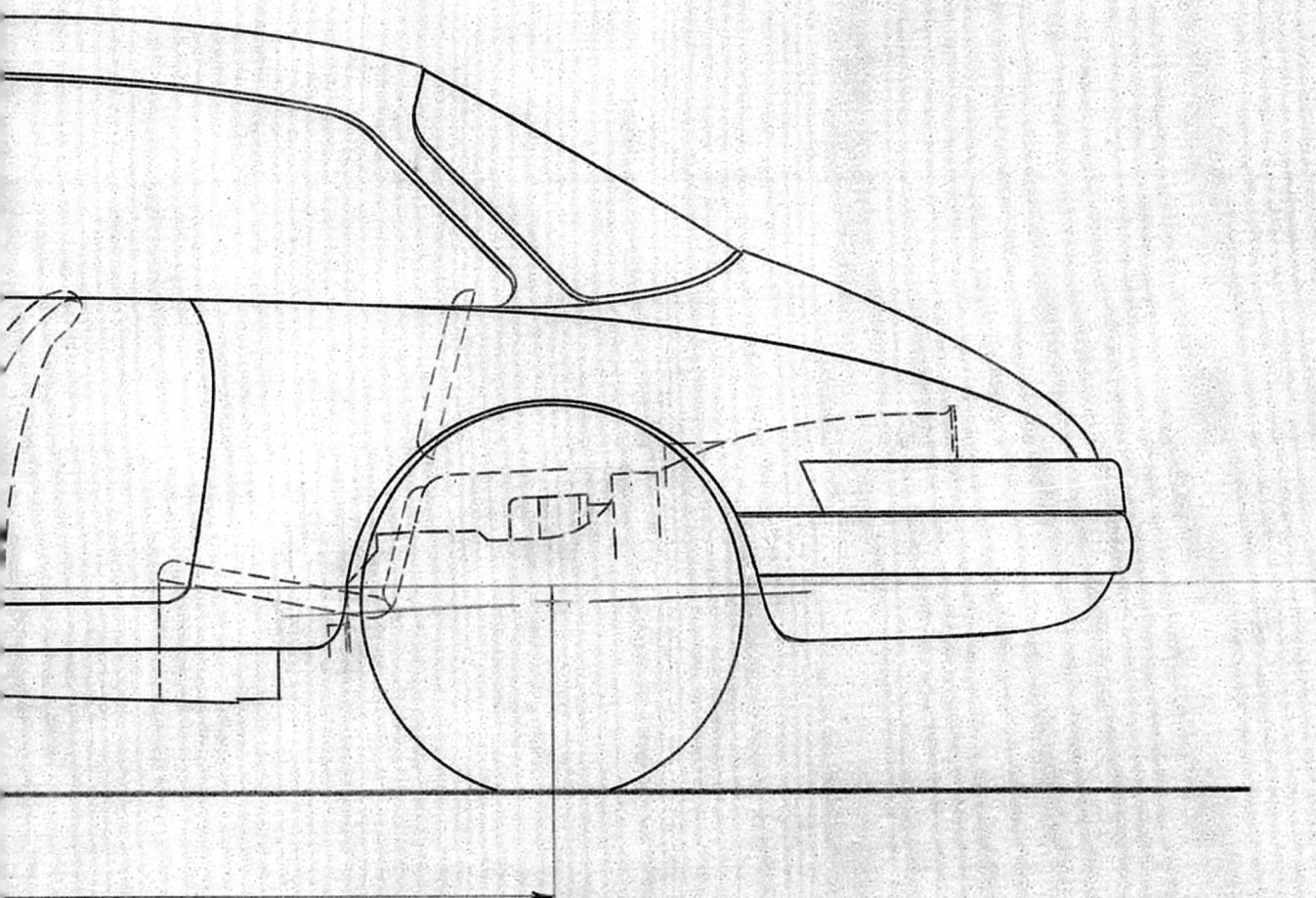

Sämtliche Abweichungen für Maße ohne Toleranzangaben				Änderungen		Tag	Name	Gepr.
Bearbeitete Flächen	Roh'stflächen		Pr.					

Urheberrecht gesetzlich geschützt!
Dr. Ing. h. c. F. Porsche K. G.
STUTTGART-ZUFFENHAUSEN

Werkstoff
Material

	Gez.	Gepr.	Gen.	Maßstab
Tag	17.11.61			1:10
Name				
Rohgewicht/St.	kg	Ersatz f.		
Fertiggewicht/St.	kg	Ersetzt d.		

Bez. *T 7 mit verlängertem Radstand*

Stck.

Z. Nr.: **695.003.505.50**

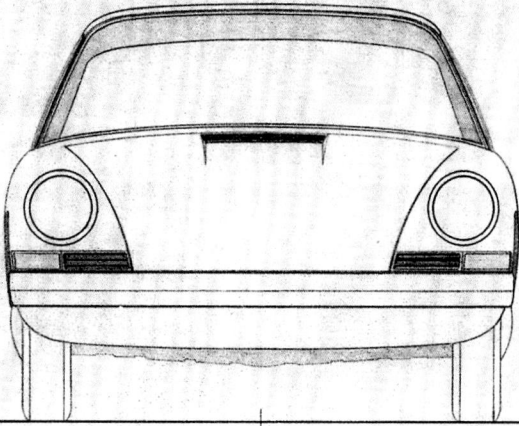

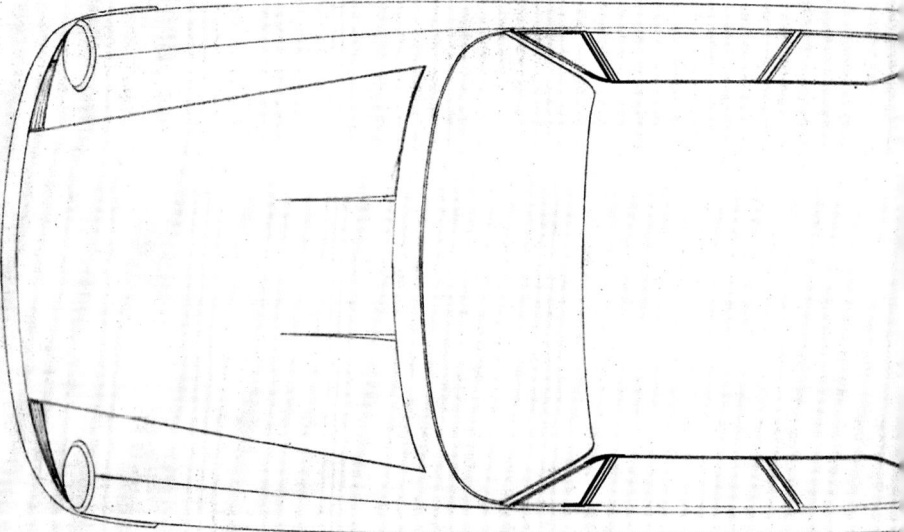

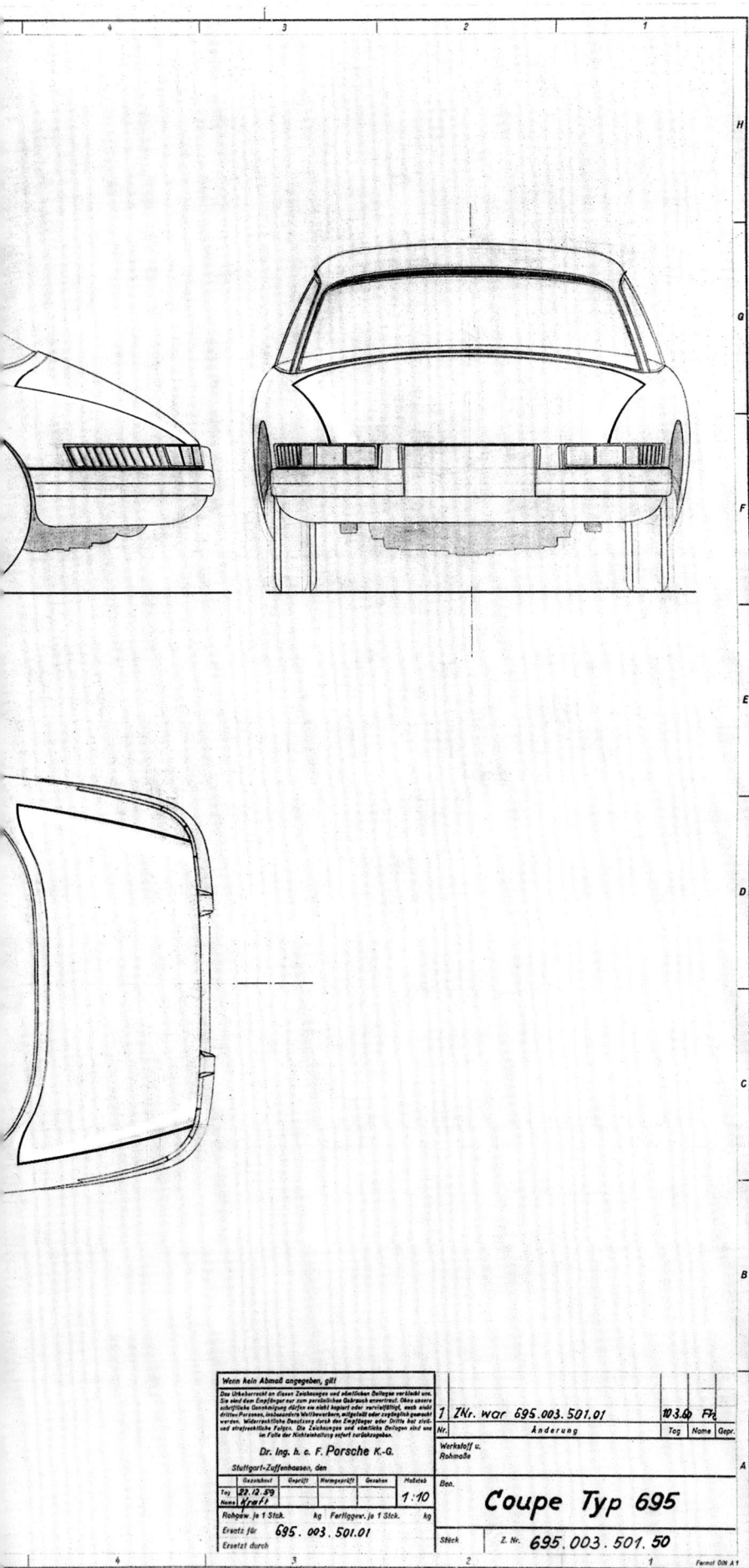

Within the technical drawing title block:

Wenn kein Abmaß angegeben, gilt

Das Urheberrecht an diesen Zeichnungen und sämtlichen Beilagen verbleibt uns.
Sie sind dem Empfänger nur zum persönlichen Gebrauch anvertraut. Ohne unsere
schriftliche Genehmigung dürfen sie nicht kopiert oder vervielfältigt, noch nicht
dritten Personen, insbesondere Wettbewerbern, mitgeteilt oder zugänglich gemacht
werden. Widerrechtliche Benutzung durch den Empfänger oder Dritte hat zivil-
und strafrechtliche Folgen. Die Zeichnungen und sämtliche Beilagen sind uns
im Falle der Nichteinhaltung sofort zurückzugeben.

Dr. Ing. h. c. F. Porsche K.-G.
Stuttgart-Zuffenhausen, den

| 1 | ZNr. war 695.003.501.01 | 10 3.60 | FP. |
| Nr. | Änderung | Tag | Name | Gepr. |

Werkstoff u.
Rohmaße

| Tag | 22.12.59 | Gezeichnet | Geprüft | Normgeprüft | Gesehen | Maßstab |
| Name | Kraft | | | | | 1:10 |

Rohgew. je 1 Stck.   kg   Fertiggew. je 1 Stck.   kg

Ersatz für   695.003.501.01
Ersetzt durch

Ben.

Coupe Typ 695

Stück   Z. Nr.   695.003.501.50

Format DIN A1

ZEICHENBEDARF H. FREYTAG, STUTTGART

---

models – and on October 9, 1959, a 1:7.5 clay model was completed and ready for inspection. F. A. Porsche later reported a remarkable timescale for the phase from initial sketches to the first clay model – all of this was allegedly completed between the end of August and the start of October. At this point, he had already been working for Porsche for two years, although his official appointment probably did not take place until 1958, verified by the fact that this is the year stated in his biography as the start of his employment at Porsche. In reality, F. A. Porsche had already been involved in a range of different projects in Stuttgart for some time. Nevertheless, the period of time in which this first form took shape is not very long – and F. A. Porsche found a form that defined some of the details of the later 901/911. All this notwithstanding, there was still a lack of clarity on how much the new car should align itself with its predecessor.

It was a process of discovery that Ferry Porsche described in German magazine *Form* (issue 27/1964) as follows: »It was five years ago that we first started to think about designing and building a new, additional car. In addition to the successful 356 model, the details of which had been continually refined over the years. We started, as usual, with the idea and, of course, the ifs and buts of the various options – is a new model even necessary? Are our customers no longer satisfied with the improved models, despite their ever-increasing performance? How would it be paid for, and what purpose will it fill? What are the costs involved, and who would be the target

THE T7 SLOWLY BEGINS TO TAKE SHAPE – AND THE FRONT END IS ALREADY THE 901.

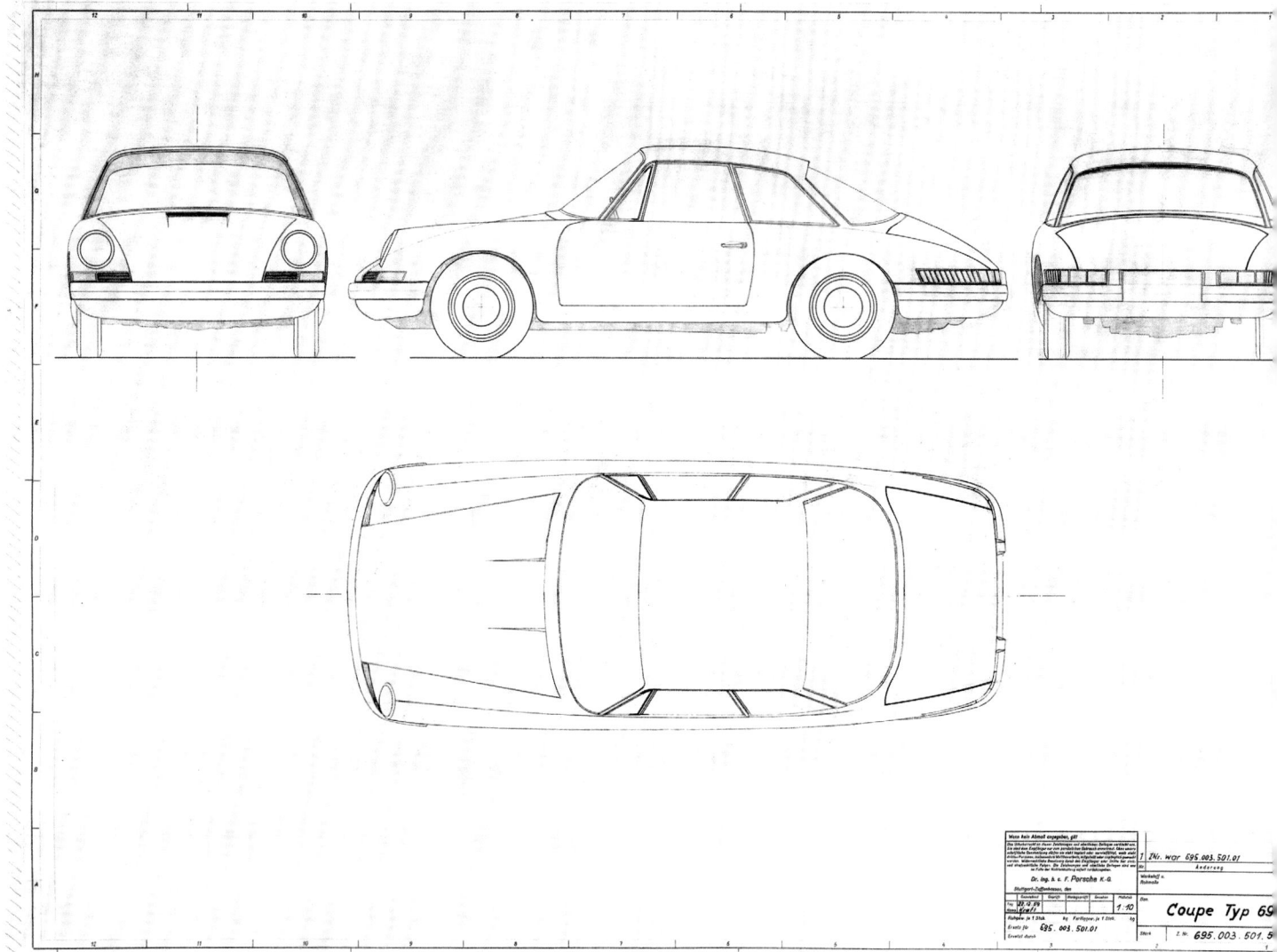

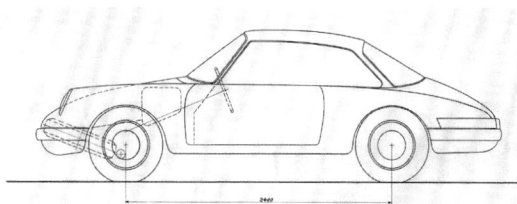

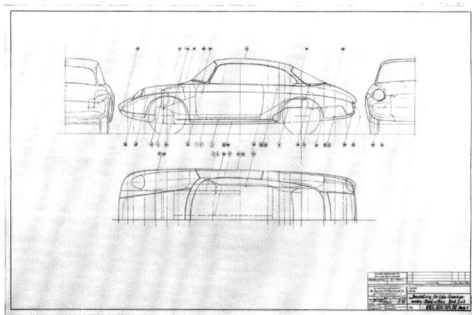

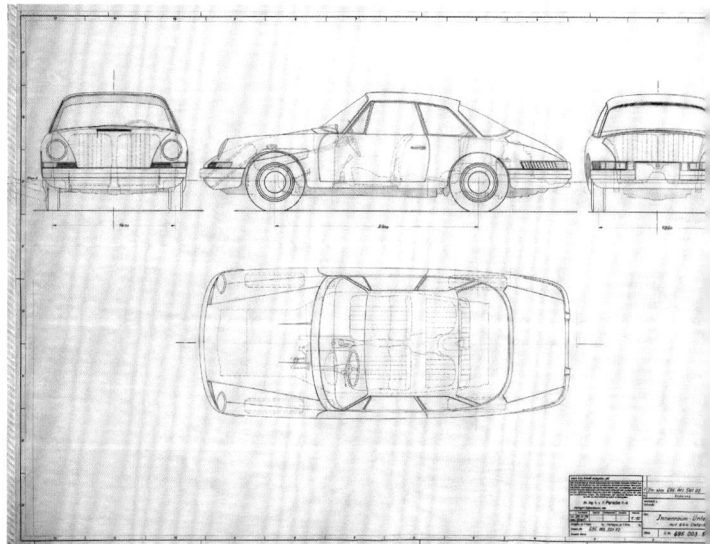

THE TYPE 695 (T7) TAKES SHAPE – CENTER LEFT IS THE DESIGN WITH THE BIG 2400 MM WHEELBASE, BESIDE IT A SKETCH SHOWING THE TECHNICAL UNDERPINNINGS OF THE T8. AN EARLY DRAWING FROM 1957 SHOWS AERODYNAMIC ECHOES OF CITROËN (BELOW LEFT).

FAHRGESTELL 754.003.301.00

ABOVE AND RIGHT IS THE T7 WITH THE NEW 754 UNDERPINNINGS VISIBLE, BELOW IT THE FIRST 695 SKETCH SUCCINCTLY ENTITLED »SPORTWAGEN«. BELOW LEFT, A DESIGN WITH A WHEELBASE OF 2375 MM – BESIDE IT, AN ALTERNATIVE WITH A 2400 MM WHEELBASE.

F. PORSCHE: WE STARTED AS USUAL WITH THE IDEA

customers? These are considerations that eventually solidify into a concept through level-headed market observation and through experience. The main requirement was to create an economical and fast vehicle that is on the same level as the Carrera 2000 GS in terms of weight and temperament, i.e. a powerful engine, lightning-fast acceleration, but nevertheless also a car for city drivers.

The first preliminary clay model was tabled for discussion in October of the same year, 1959. One year later, following wind tunnel testing, we had the first drivable car for road testing. But this was when the first doubts set in on whether or not we should stick to the concept. The engineers were calling for a longer wheelbase, and we had to correct our initial thoughts that the owner would not transport household goods with a luxurious

vehicle like this. The outcome was a new front axle construction for a larger luggage compartment, making the car a true 2+2-seater. New constructions and new models followed. Until, in November 1962, the first styling model, built from wood and metal in 1:1 scale, locked down the final design.

The new bodyshell form is even more aerodynamic than the type 356. The longer wheelbase delivered the called-for spacious interior, particularly the increased legroom for rear-seat passengers. In spite of its wider interior, the car actually became narrower by 70 mm due to reductions in its bulging side cross-sections. Larger doors now make it considerably easier to climb into and out of the rear seats. In contrast to previous models, the front fenders can be detached for any necessary repair work. The air-cooled, two-liter, six-cylinder boxer engine with 130 hp delivers a top speed of 210 km/h. We want to start production of this new, additional car in the fall.«

When you read this statement from 1964, you could be forgiven for believing that the good people of Zuffenhausen had originally planned a new model with the same wheelbase as the 356, then subsequently extended it. But, in actual fact, this first model was built on a wheelbase of 240 centimeters, although relatively quickly shortened by ten centimeters. The reason for this lay in the realization that the proportions would run out of control, which is why the final wheelbase was ultimately set at 230 centimeters.

Because the model immediately received a great deal of positive feedback, the decision was taken relatively quickly to build a 1:1 model – a task that

THE T7 WAS BUILT BETWEEN DECEMBER 1959 AND SUMMER 1960 UNDER THE MODEL DESIGNATION 754.

THE T7 CLAY MODEL IN 1:7.5 SCALE WAS BUILT IN OCTOBER 1959 ON A PLANNED WHEELBASE OF 240 CENTIMETERS.

SUMMER 1960 SAW THE COMPLETION OF A HAND-BUILT T7 – THE PHOTO OF THE ENGINE COMPARTMENT WAS TAKEN LATER, AS INDICATED BY THE REAR-MOUNTED CARRERA POWER UNIT.

PORSCHE TOOK 13 MONTHS TO COMPLETE THE FIRST DRIVABLE T7 – THE TWO INSTRUMENT DIALS ARE VISIBLE ON THE DASHBOARD.

AND
ONCE
AGAIN
THE
WHEELBASE
WAS
SHORTENED

the rear end – never before had this much daylight managed to fight its way into a Porsche interior, and rearward visibility also took a massive leap forward.

While the team in Zuffenhausen began building the 1:1 model, the 1:7.5 one made its way to the Technical University of Stuttgart, where work began immediately on testing the aerodynamics in the wind tunnel and on detail optimization.

As Ferry Porsche confirmed in his article in *Form*, the next 13 months saw the construction of a drivable prototype of the T7, which entered Porsche history as the type 754. And on November 1, 1960, Helmuth Bott, then Head of Test Driving and later Board member for Technical Development, was able to undertake his first drive in the type 754. After the first few kilometers, the critical engineer climbed out of the car and astonished the group waiting expectantly with the words, »We can forget that car!«, although he was actually referring less to the vehicle itself and more to the all-new, two-liter six-cylinder, which was mounted in the rear as an underfloor engine.

AFTER HIS FIRST DRIVE WITH THE T7, HELMUTH BOTT ANNOUNCED: »WE CAN FORGET THAT CAR!«

was completed in a very short space of time, as just under three months later, on December 28, a full-size T7 appeared mounted on a wooden frame. What is interesting is that Ferdinand Alexander Porsche had already so clearly defined the front end with this first design that it subsequently appeared in the 901 with just a few minor modifications. The rear end, on the other hand, was still very different from the later series-production version. In the interests of giving more headroom to rear-seat passengers, F. A. Porsche had added a distinct offset and notch to the classic fastback, setting this design clearly apart from the familiar Porsche form. However, he later admitted that the notch in the rear end was insufficient to provide rear-seat passengers with the necessary headroom. »The notch was a compromise between more headroom and aesthetics – we accepted the restricted seating height in the back.« Another surprising factor was the more than generous amount of glass around

As an experienced engineer and chassis man, Bott of course knew perfectly well that it would be possible to address most of the prototype's problems with detail refinements. But he also knew enough to recognize clearly when an engine was a complete lemon – which was obviously the case here. What had been developed for the new car was an engine that simply would not fulfill the requirements stated by Ferry Porsche. Stuttgart took the decision to go with an underfloor engine because this extremely flat construction could have been mounted so low in the back that there would still have been room above it for a luggage compartment, thus fulfilling the customer desire for more luggage space. From that standpoint, the initial idea of using this kind of engine was fully appropriate – and to go with a two-liter displacement and six cylinders also made sense. And if any thought was given to using an eight-cylinder – because work was also ongoing at the time on type 753 and 771 eight-cylinder boxer engines for motorsport applications – it rapidly became apparent that these motors would be considered far too complicated and too expensive for everyday use.

NGINE OF THE TYPE 745 WAS EVER BUILT — HELMUTH BOTT DESCRIBED IT AS »UNDRIVEABLE«.

THE
745 ENGINE
SHOULD
NEVER
HAVE
BEEN
BUILT

engine would be high-revving and have large valves and a relatively narrow construction. However, he supplemented these sensible dimensions with a rather bulky and antiquated camshaft control system – two central camshafts used long pushrods to control the overhead valves, which were arranged in a V formation. The two camshafts were driven by shafts rotating at half the speed of the crankshaft, with the upper camshaft controlling the intake valves and the lower camshaft the exhaust valves. Obviously one can ask the question today why the development team back then chose to stick with this technology, despite the fact that it was already apparent from the 356 engine that it had reached the end of its useful life in terms of engine revving and running characteristics.

On one side, there were rumors that Claus von Rücker was still comfortable with this technology from his time at Studebaker. However, this type of valve control also appeared in a similar form in the eight-cylinder grand prix engines – although the camshaft drive gears were not located at the flywheel (as in a grand prix engine), but at the front end of the crankshaft. Ultimately, this design did actually result in a pretty flat layout – also helped by the unconventional positioning of the cooling fans. There were two fans, each driven by its own belt running on the end of the crankshaft and each supplying one cylinder bank with cooling air. Obviously, these two externally arranged axial fans were smaller than the previously used large central fan, and they delivered the required additional centimeters of space.

In his book *Porsche – Excellence was Expected*, Karl Ludvigsen also describes the mixture formation. »Carburetors were arrayed along the left and right flanks of the flat six, where they fed the ›side-draft‹ inlet ports. According to Porsche records the ports were fed experimentally with horizontal Solex floatless carburetors. Visible on a surviving Type 745, however, were the individual downdraft Solex carburetors that were normally used (mounted on curved inlet stubs). An electric fuel pump was fitted. This novel six-cylinder engine was tested on the dynamometer and in the Porsche 695 in 1962. With a 9.5:1 compression ratio it produced 120 bhp at 6,500 rpm in its original two-liter form and 123 pound-feet of torque. Because that was not quite the level of power that was desired the engine was also run in an enlarged 2,195 cc version, achieved by expanding the bore to 84 mm. The larger displacement delivered the sought-after 130 bhp at 6,500 rpm and 130 pound-feet of torque – nice round numbers from an engine which, because of its long pushrods, could never be run at appreciably higher crankshaft speeds. Hence the flat six would not have been adaptable to competition use.«

Claus von Rücker, on whose watch this six-cylinder – known as the type 745 – was created, called for a somewhat strange engine layout. On the one hand, he opted for an oversquare variant with a large 60 mm bore and a short stroke of 66 mm. This ensured that the boxer

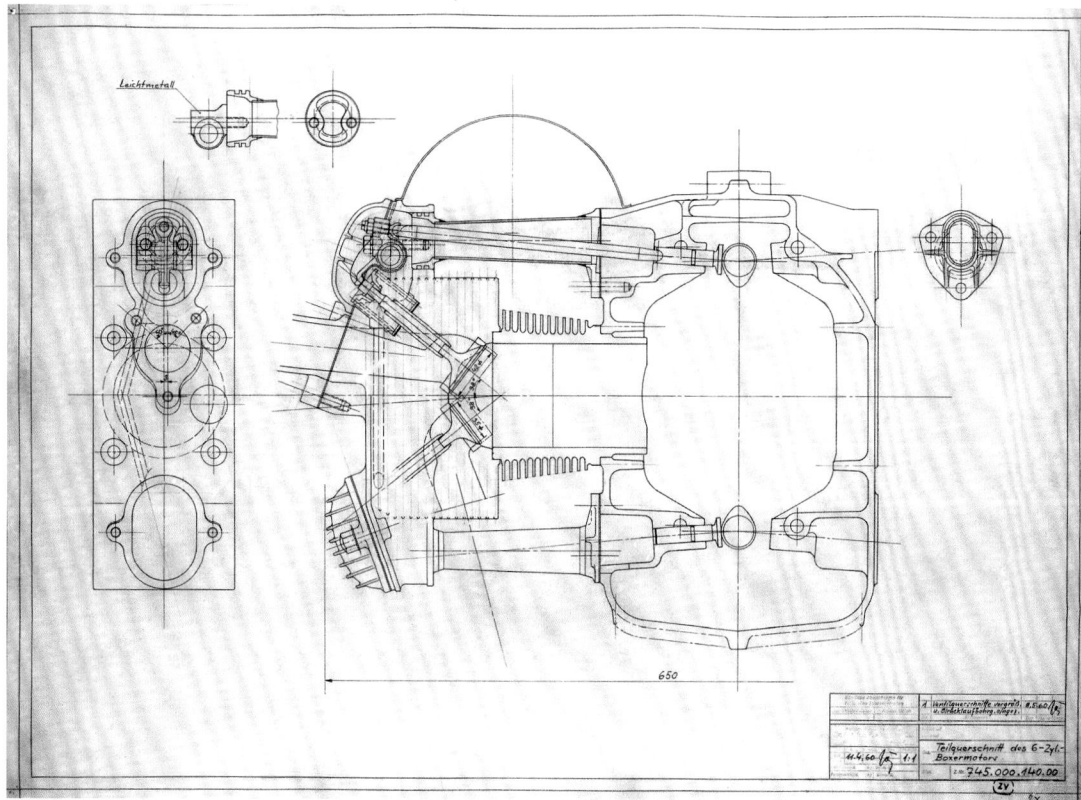

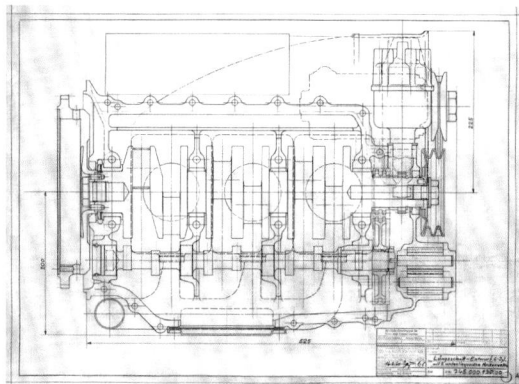

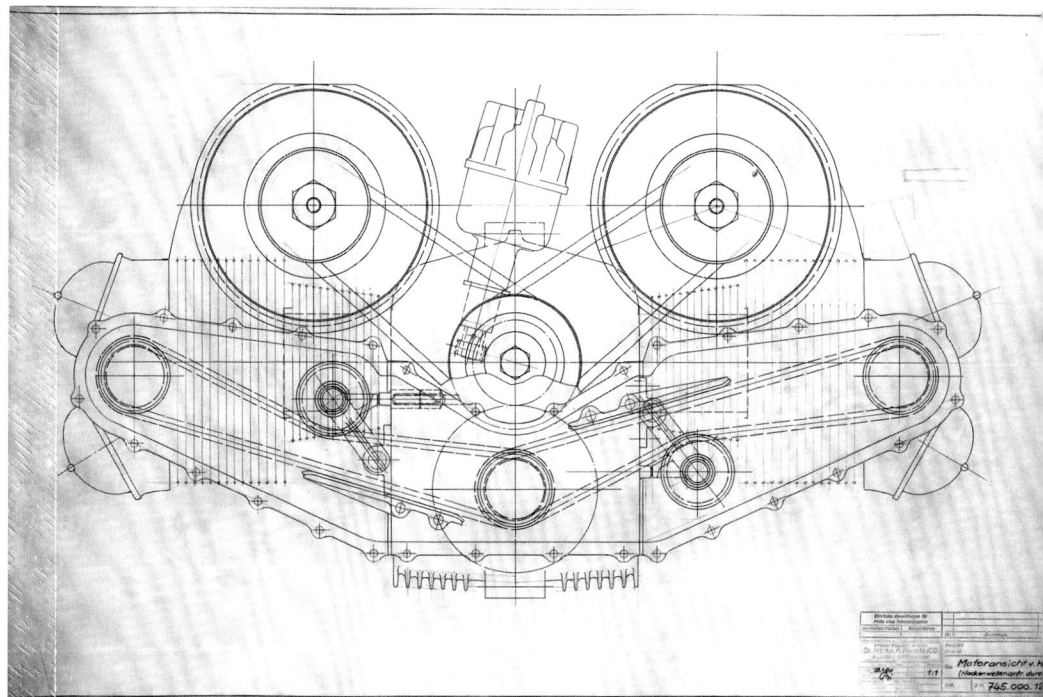

THE TWO OUTER COOLING FANS MAY HAVE PROVIDED A LOW INSTALLATION HEIGHT, BUT THE VALVE CONTROL WAS ANTIQUATED, FEATURING LONG PUSHRODS AND TWO CAMSHAFTS MOUNTED ABOVE AND BELOW THE CRANKSHAFT.

This was an opinion that Hans Mezger shares to this day. »The engine was very close to the design from which we wanted to move away,« says Mezger, referring to the four-cylinder boxer engine in the Porsche 356. »It was a six-cylinder boxer with a two-liter displacement. It was supposed to generate the power achieved by the four-cylinder Fuhrmann engine in its final evolution as a road-going version with a two-liter displacement – 130 hp. But it did not run on the test stand for long«, says Mezger, because it quickly became evident that this was not the way to achieve the objective. 120 hp at 6500 rpm was less than had been hoped for. The crankshaft bearings and valve drive limited the power increases achievable through higher engine speeds. And when Claus von Rücker then left Porsche in 1962 to be replaced by Hans Tomala, it became clear that the six-cylinder type 745 was completely dead in the water.

And thus it came to be that this engine was mothballed right after its first outing – a decision that was accelerated not just by the assessment handed down by Helmuth Bott after his drive in the 754, but also by the opinion of co-workers, who obviously knew very well where the engine's weaknesses lay.

Most of the test driving, however, took place with a Carrera 2 series-production engine. Although the highly complex, 130 hp four-cylinder with its four overhead camshafts, dual ignition and dry-sump lubrication, offered more than sufficient zest for the task, it was clear to all at Porsche that this engine was not the solution they were looking for – the work it took to keep it running drove even hardened mechanics to distraction. It is worth mentioning that, in order to achieve more power output, Claus von Rücker then also worked on a four-cylinder push-rod engine from the 356 with Kugelfischer fuel injection. But this project, with the model designation 616, met with a relatively quick end as well.

However, aside from the disappointment with the engine, the type 754 did not look all that bad. Admittedly, the initial running gear still came from the 356 – the trailing-arm axle at the front and the familiar swing-arm axle at the rear – and Helmuth Bott and his fellow combatants were well aware of their particular idiosyncrasies. A McPherson strut arrangement was also tested at the front. This not only saved space, it was also simple and inexpensive. As a further development of double wishbone suspension, the upper control arm is left out and wheel control transferred in part to the damper. It ends at the top with the so-called dome bearing, which allows the whole damper to turn. The coil springs also pivot fully with steering movements. Paul Frère wrote in his definitive work *The Porsche 911 Story*, »This allowed the space-consuming coil springs to be replaced by torsion bars. The latter sat in the tubular base of the control arm, solidly fixed to its front end.«

The type 7 was driven a total of just 1600 kilometers and then abandoned in a storage room, which was

A NICE LITTLE GET-TOGETHER:
(R. TO L.) FRANZ XAVER REIMSPIESS,
LEOPOLD SCHMID, ERWIN KOMENDA,
LOUISE PIËCH, KARL RABE.

actually a pity, as the 754 offered significantly more interior space than the 356 and looked a good deal more modern. German enthusiast magazine *Motor Klassik* wrote in a report on the car, which was restored and made drivable once more by Porsche after have been forgotten for decades, »With the broad and extensively glazed architecture of the roof resting on delicate pillars, the design stands in direct contrast to the introverted character of the rotund 356, whose windshields look like observation slits in comparison.

TODAY, THE T7 IS SEEN AS THE FATHER OF THE 911

ONLY ONE UNIT OF THE T7 WAS EVER BUILT — IT WAS REJECTED AFTER JUST 1600 KILOMETERS.

PAGE 072

But the bright interior space is deceiving. It gives the impression of more width than is actually available – as proven by an attempt to sit in the two rear seats. It is possible for one person to sit here – albeit only a short person traveling for an equally short distance. This is not sufficient to elevate a 2+2 coupe to a four-seater. Plus, there was no room for luggage. The space beneath the front hood was already largely filled by the spare wheel and the fuel tank. Weekend luggage for two would barely fit into this – so why bother with four seats?«

Yet the T7 is rightly seen today as the father of the 911 – its front end with its freestanding headlamps and hood sloping elegantly downward already defines the face of later generations. On the inside, the evolution of the dashboard is clearly evident – even if there are just two dials in the driver's field of vision providing information on the car's status. And the large glass areas provide the first indication of a departure from the rather rudimentary looking windows of the 356 – the rear end is still not quite right, the small air intakes left and right in the rear fenders still look rather contrived and the notch in the rear end still disturbs the aesthetic in the eye of the beholder, who has been used to admiring the rounded curve of the 356. But these were all minor details – the development of the 901/911 now gathered speed. The foundations had been laid – Ferry Porsche was now able to approve the design and development of the T7 successor. But this is when something unusual happened. On the one side, development boss Erwin Komenda set about pushing forward with the T7 in line with his own thinking, a development that would bear the internal model designation T9. In parallel, Ferdinand Alexander Porsche began turning his ideas into a model of his own, the T8. We will never know whether this was played out freely in line with the Olympic motto »may the best man win«. However, it certainly appears to be the case that the self-confident Chief Engineer Komenda, who had worked for Ferdinand senior and his son Ferry Porsche since 1931, was of the impression that he would of course retain the upper hand with this car, too – just like with the Beetle, 356 and 904 before it. This was an evaluation of the situation, however, that would take an unexpected turn with the arrival in the company of the young and ambitious sons of the Porsche and Piëch families.

ALTHOUGH THE T7 MAY HAVE LOOKED SPACIOUS, IT WAS IN REALITY MORE OF A TWO-SEATER WITH ROOM FOR TWO SMALL CHILDREN IN THE BACK. BUT IT SHOWED THE DIRECTION THAT PORSCHE WOULD NOW TAKE.

T7 + T8 = 901

BUT THE T9 WAS A BIT OF A *PROBLEM*

Ferry Porsche had already stated many times what he wanted from his 356 successor: more interior – more power – less costly production – no horrifically expensive and hard-to-maintain »Fuhrmann« engine. After all the trials and tribulations, the T7 seemed to be the right approach. But now the concept had to be refined and production-engineered. The task was now to mold the T7 into the right shape and, in parallel, prepare it for series production – that the right engine had not yet been found, however, added something of a complication to the development process. However, the company was not one to put all its eggs in one basket – starting in early 1960, two teams were working relatively independently of one another to take the T7 to the next level. On the one side there was F. A. Porsche, the man who was supposed to perfect the shape, and, on the other, was Erwin Komenda, who, as one of Ferry Porsche's most trusted inner circle, had to take care of the engineering.

In order to understand what happened then, one should take a quick look at the history. Born in 1904, Komenda was Lead Engineer in the Bodyshell Test and Development department at Daimler-Benz AG in Stuttgart-Sindelfingen from 1929 until 1931, as well as Deputy Head of the Production Engineering department. Prior to that, he had worked since 1927 for Steyr in Austria as a bodyshell engineer. This is where he met and gained the trust of Ferdinand Porsche. After the latter had set himself up in business with his »Konstruktionsbüro für Motoren-, Fahrzeug-, Luftfahrzeug- und Wasserfahrzeugbau« (Design Office for Engine, Vehicle, Aircraft and Watercraft Engineering) on December 1, 1930 he hired Komenda one year later. And this is where he stayed for 35 years until 1966, working as Chief Bodyshell Engineer for Porsche senior and Porsche junior. Erwin Komenda was responsible for vehicle equipment, as well as costing, work preparation, timing control and works planning. It is hardly surprising that this worthy man had

a well-developed sense of self and was absolutely certain that he held the full confidence of Ferry Porsche.

The situation became more complicated as the sons of the two Porsche and Piëch lines began to work their way into the family business – and the Porsche 901/911 was created precisely during this phase of company reorientation. The accomplished grandsons of Professor Ferdinand Porsche joined the company, took over the management of development projects and occupied leading positions within the company. Ferdinand Alexander »Butzi« Porsche, who was the third male Porsche scion to bear the name Ferdinand, established himself with the formation of a new design studio. Hans-Peter Porsche joined the company in 1963 and became Head of Production in 1965. Ferdinand Piëch, born out of the marriage between Louise Porsche and Anton Piëch, achieved an engineering degree from the ETH Zürich and began his professional career on April 1, 1963 working for the Race Engine Testing department. Piëch was, of course, already fully acquainted with the company and familiar with all of its projects, having worked for several summers in Zuffenhausen as an intern.

This brought about changes to the long-established structures and hierarchies at Porsche and also had a powerful influence on the evolutionary history of the Porsche type 901/911. In fact, against this background, it was possible to build a fascinating psychological profile of the different characters of all the development engineers involved in the process. It is no wonder that there was friction and irritation – and the T9, which Komenda as Chief Engineer developed to his own tastes on the basis of the T7, also played its role in this. It did not meet with the approval of family members for which Komenda had hoped.

One of the reasons for this surely lay in the fact that the Chief Engineer looked at his T9 not only as a technician, but sought also to take on the role of Chief Designer. His position was naturally understandable – he was, at the time, also the pro forma senior designer at Porsche. Ferry Porsche wrote in his memoirs on the subject, »We commissioned Mr. Komenda to build a few prototypes on the basis of the type 7 – variants 1, 2, and 3 – and, lo and behold, the cars

THE T9 ALSO PLAYED ITS PART IN THE FRICTION AND IRRITATION, ATTRACTING, AS IT DID, NO APPROVAL FROM WITHIN THE FAMILY.

ERWIN KOMENDA'S T9 WAS NOT TO THE FAMILY'S TASTE – THE REAR END IN PARTICULAR WAS HEAVILY CRITICIZED.

became ever bigger and heavier. So I intervened, limited the wheelbase to 2.20 meters and set some specifications for the suspension and the engine. You see, everything that exceeded 2.20 meters automatically led to a four-seater. I then realized that Mr. Komenda did not follow my suggestions, but was instead determined to build the cars that he and his men had designed. Moreover, he consistently changed my son's styling to reflect the tastes and preferences of himself and his team.«

The result of this independent perspective on the future model was ready for consideration at the end of January 1961. The model was more than simply a deviation from the dimensional specifications – Komenda was still of the opinion that the new model should have considerably more space for the occupants – the design evolution had also removed it significantly from the aesthetics of the T7. The T9 still had the slanting headlamps in the fenders, and nothing had been changed on the hood – but the front bumper with its uninspired indicator lamps was strangely displaced within the design (almost pushed inward), detracting a great deal from the charm and elegance of the front end. The rear end was even stranger, with its air intake and outlet grilles too wide and prominent along the length of the engine cover. Tobias Aichele describes the T9 model as »clumsy and unharmonious« in his book *Porsche Raritäten*.

It is hardly surprising that Ferry Porsche had his own opinion of the model and the situation within the company. »In the course of this disagreement, I have observed that a bodyshell engineer is not necessarily an expert when it comes to styling and, vice versa, a styling man cannot necessarily be considered an expert in the field of bodyshell design. Both, however, are convinced that they are experts in both disciplines. I now saw myself confronted with the issue of what to do in order to retain the integrity of a model as envisaged by the styling people once it lands in the hands of bodyshell engineers. I had to think of something.« And Ferry Porsche found a solution.

But let us turn first to the T8, the alternative to Erwin Komenda's model. In parallel to his T9, F. A. Porsche had also set about once again redesigning and developing the T7 in order to bring it more into line with the specifications set by his boss and father. In contrast to Komenda, however, F. A. Porsche had understood that there was no longer room in the future for a separation of design and engineering. He brought two engineers into his team in the persons of Theo Bauer and Werner Trenkler – two experienced men who constantly advised on whether the ideas put on paper by the Design department could actually be implemented in technical reality. This approach was to help him avoid running up any engineering dead-ends – it led to the doors between the design and engineering functions being more open than could ever be imagined today.

The big names of Porsche Development still recall to this day that it was standard practice every evening – before heading for home – to call into the design studio one or two floors below to take a look at the new ideas dreamed up by the design team. »And, of course, the engineers never missed an opportunity to say ›but you can't make it like that‹. With this support

THE LINE OF THE T7 WAS DEVELOPED INTO THE T8 WITH THIS INITIAL 1:1.75 MODEL.

078

from Helmuth Bott, Valentin Schäffer or Hans Mezger – to name just a few – it was possible to avoid some of the pitfalls. These visits were also a welcome diversion from other everyday responsibilities. F. A. Porsche obviously benefited from the suggestions that were brought to him week after week – and he did not shy away from marching into the engineering office above with the same confidence if he got stuck with anything. The problem would then be discussed in detail and both sides looked for a solution together that would satisfy the aesthetics and the engineering to the same degree.

Work on the T8 progressed at speed and led to a slew of 1:7.5 scale clay models that clarified how the form of the 901 was slowly beginning to crystallize out of the T7. Reinhard Seiffert wrote extensively about this design process in German magazine *Motor Revue* (issue 51): ›Ferry Porsche had always been of the opinion that it would be quite all right for a second Porsche to resemble the first one. But there was nevertheless plenty of fresh motivation, because it is not just fashion that changes, but generations, too. The man who was once a Porsche junior has long become a Porsche senior, and the Porsche junior of the moment – also called Ferdinand – has discovered the discipline of design. Industrial design, once more or less incidental, has now become a complex in its

own right, be it kitchen appliances or cars. Ferry Porsche is very relaxed about this development, because he assumes that a form that makes sense can never be bad. But he left it to Porsche junior to work out the lines of the new car.‹

And Porsche junior had no easy time of it. ›It is easier to work for other companies than for your own,‹ he says. There were opinions and counter-opinions – the process also involved the fundamental question of whether a Porsche really needs to look like a Porsche, leading to the design of notchback models. That was around the time of the four-seater experiment, with the rearward flowing roofline delivering more headroom for those seated in the rear. The two-seater concept, however, retains the ›Porsche‹ rear. The decision was taken that the new car would indeed look like a Porsche.«

And that is probably the major step forward in the evolution of the 901 from the form of the T7. The classic fastback was back in – and, with the silhouette of the 901, F. A. Porsche created a distinctive line that can only be described as simply perfect. Even half a century after it was penned, this model still does not look old. On the contrary, in fact, the years appear only to have added to its class. It comes as no surprise that collectors have discovered the early models and that prices for these classics continue to sky rocket. But Ferdinand Alexander Porsche was tasked not only with finding the line – which he achieved with instinctive dexterity – but also with uniting this form with the necessary technology and ergonomic demands.

THE FIRST 1:1 MODEL OF THE T8 CLEARLY SHOWS THAT THE 901 WAS NOW TANTALIZINGLY CLOSE.

There was still more than enough for his team to do, as Reinhard Seiffert explains, »Large window surfaces and low waistlines were demands that not only took account of changes in tastes, but that also increased visibility. More length and less width meant new overall proportions – an improvement, in fact, as the type 356 is a little too wide for its length. The call was to gain as much interior and luggage space as possible and, above all, to retain the wheelbase of 2.20 m set in stone by Ferry Porsche. There was no lack of underlings keen to secure a few more centimeters, but the boss was resolute. ›The car will be crammed full at 2.20 m,‹ he said, ›and just as crammed full at 2.40 m. So let's just stick with 2.20 m.‹ He was certainly right in his assessment that the car would be crammed full. There is virtually not a single corner that is not used to the maximum. Nevertheless, they exceeded expectations and indeed created more interior and luggage space than in the 356. But there were further practical considerations – removable front fenders (to reduce

THERE WERE THOUGHTS OF A TARGA AS FAR BACK AS 1962

IT WOULD BE ANOTHER FIVE YEARS BEFORE THE TARGA BECAME REALITY.

the cost of bodyshell repairs); bumpers that butt up to the bodyshell, yet have a travel of several centimeters in the event of an impact without damaging the bodyshell; easier access to the rear bench (hence the angled window posts); direct ventilation for the front brakes. It is no wonder that it took several years for the car to reach its final form.«

Despite his excellent contacts with Porsche (the Editor-in-Chief of *auto motor und sport* would later be Editor-in-Chief of *Christophorus* for many years), Reinhard Seiffert was naturally not in possession of all the details. The preparations and investigations that led to the T7 may well have taken all those years, but it was also because Ferry Porsche did not put an end to all the debate concerning the size of the interior until very late in the process. However, the evolution of the T7 happened in a comparatively short space of time, as they wanted to present the car in September 1963 at the Frankfurt Motor Show and commence series production a short time later. The reason for the hurry was, on the one side, that it was becoming increasingly evident that the 356 was slowly approaching the end of its model life – compared with the competition, it was lacking in spirit and comfort. And, on the other side, this very small company was starting to feel the pain of the development costs – a rapid market launch was required to generate new revenue streams. All this led to the completion on April 16, 1962 of an initial, not yet drivable, 1:1 model made from metal, wood and glass that would serve as a reference model for all the decision makers.

Let us now return to Ferry Porsche and his ruminations on how to solve the problems between his Chief Engineer Erwin Komenda and his son – he wrote in his memoirs, »I had to think of something. By this time, we had taken over the company Reutter, which had its own in-house engineering department. So I went to

Mr. Beierbach, who was Managing Director of Reutter at the time, and I said to him, ›Mr. Beierbach, here is the model my son made. Could you have it drawn up just as it is?‹ Mr. Beierbach was indeed able to do that, and had the model rendered as engineering drawings. When Mr. Komenda heard about this he was initially flabbergasted, but he came round after a few weeks and ultimately started to pull in the preferred direction. He and his department now also started to produce drawings. The ultimate outcome was what was already standing in the Styling department as a 1:1 model – the 901. Reutter then transferred over the form unchanged, although he first discussed with me one or two things that were current at the time. It was actually some time later before they were all realized: things like a large rear window in the 901 that could be opened in order to load bags. Neither Mr. Beierbach nor Mr. Komenda were sufficiently confident to take that on at the time.«

With the decision to give the type 8 to Reutter to have it drawn up, Ferry Porsche had not only shown a preference for his son's design, he had also showed Erwin Komenda that he had to adapt to the changing times. One can also read into the statement »But he came round after a few weeks and ultimately started to pull in the preferred direction« that Komenda needed some time to accept the solution.

The basis for the 901 was finally set in stone – and the engineers set about giving the new vehicle the technical underpinnings necessary for series production. On a separate note, this was also the time to resolve once and for all the matter of the engine, which was back on the table following the false start with the original underfloor type 745 motor.

All at Porsche were clear that the second attempt should naturally also be made with an air-cooled power unit positioned at the rear – Ferry Porsche talked about this in a conversation with Reinhard Seiffert, »We are not married either to the air cooling or the rear positioning of the engine – at the end of the day, the twelve-cylinder in the Cisitalia was water cooled. On the other hand, the Porsche name now carries with it a certain expectation, from which one should deviate only with good reason. Because our vehicles are always used in motorsport, too, where they are expected to be successful, the 901

A CLEAR DECISION — THE MID ENGINE IS USED IN RACING CARS LIKE THE 904 CARRERA GTS,
WHILE THE REAR ENGINE IS RESERVED FOR THE GT.

THE
901
CONCEPT
WAS
UNAVOIDABLE

concept was more or less unavoidable. You see, a competitive sports car calls for such a degree of weight on the driven wheels that separating the location of the engine from that of the drive was simply out of the question. The mid engine – as the ideal engine location for pure race cars – is out of the question for GT cars because it places too much restriction on the interior space. And front-wheel drive is also not an option, because it is unable to deliver such a large amount of power to the road effectively, resulting in a lot of wheel spin. What we are then left with is putting the engine at the rear axle.«

During this interview, Ferry Porsche also stated his opinion on the future of manufacturers that built front-engine cars for motorsport. »In future, they will have to build mid-engine vehicles, as the example of Ferrari already shows. This will mean major design deviations between series-production and competition vehicles. Porsche, on the other hand, can drive either with its standard rear-engine vehicle, or simply turn the unit around. Placing the engine in front of the rear axle is, of course, better for handling characteristics – that's why the 904 competition car was derived from the 901 road car. However, I am certain that the handling characteristics of the 901 will be so good that it will always be able to compete as a GT with front-engine cars, perhaps even with mid-engine cars. In any event, we will use the same engine for both layouts.«

A SUCCESSFUL TRIO – JOAKIM BONNIER, HERBERT LINGE AND HELMUTH BOTT (L. TO R.)
AT THE 1000-KM RACE AT THE NÜRBURGRING ON MAY 31, 1964.

It is unclear whether, during the design process, any thought went into a construction other than the boxer – Reinhard Seiffert nevertheless spoke about such thinking in his article in *Motor Revue*. »The plan to develop an engine that could easily be used in front of and behind the rear axle also played a major role in the conception phase. Because, for the time being, one remains tied to the piston engine,

»THE HANDLING CHARACTERISTICS OF THE 901 WILL BE SO GOOD THAT IT WILL ALWAYS BE COMPETITIVE.«

the fundamental options on offer were the inline engine, V engine and boxer engine. The inline engine only makes sense for a rear-engine layout when it is mounted transversely. This calls for redirecting the power flow twice using spur gears, with its associated added noise and friction. A short-stroke, inline six-cylinder would be quite long and therefore unsuitable for transverse mounting. Six cylinders were, however, a fundamental requirement, as increasing the displacement would benefit both comfort and sporting performance. Six short-stroke cylinders would create the necessary prerequisites for high revving (the thinking being around 9000 rpm).

A V engine would be ideal for a mid-engine layout; stretching it to 180 degrees, i.e. a boxer engine, would be better for a rear-engine layout. On this point, Ferry Porsche is utterly convinced by the fundamentals once adopted by his father in conceiving the VW. This also applies to the cooling: Porsche considers it senseless to cool a boxer engine with water. The inevitable cavities between the cylinders and bisection of the block are perfect for air cooling. Plus, there is the necessity to keep the weight of an engine mounted behind the rear axle as low as possible.

Another factor, of course, is the enormous amount of experience gained in air cooling at Porsche. There was no fear of heat problems and they had already proven that the noise disadvantage could more or less be eliminated. Porsche also puts forward theoretical benefits: Air cooling consumes less power because the heat differential between the (hotter) air-cooled cylinders and the ambient air is greater. Without a doubt, however, the balance was tipped by practical considerations.«

»At the end of the 1950s, the mood for change here was amazing,« recalls Hans Mezger in a lengthy interview with the magazine *Porsche Fahrer* (Porsche Driver). Business was going well, they were working on entering

Formula 1 and, in parallel, had begun work on a successor to the Porsche 356 – and after the 745 project failed, the engine man joined the engine development team in 1963. Mezger now reckons that the end of the Formula 1 project was also connected to the unsatisfactory development of the new series-production engine for the 356 successor. »There were a number of attempts that had not brought the desired success.« Thus, the focus of the company turned to the development of the new power unit, especially as time was running out. In April 1962, Hans Tomala took over from Claus von Rücker and there was a certain pressure to consider fundamental change. It was during these months that the decision was taken to redesign the 745 engine completely – although the general layout and main specifications were retained. There was no change in stroke, bore, displacement or cylinder spacing – however, some details of the type 821 (the designation of this engine) had to be changed at a later point. Hans Mezger reckons that »the preference was to retain the existing casting molds for the crankcase for reasons of cost«. Thus, the molds for the type 821 were redesigned in order to take into account the technical requirements of the new design. »We paid close attention to costs at Porsche.« The 821 engine was to become the link between the failed 745 and the future 901 engine – it was completed in early 1963 and its key advance was in the repositioning of the previously central camshafts into the two cylinder heads. For the development engineers, it was clear that only overhead camshafts would deliver the reliability and sporty layout that Ferry Porsche was expecting. »There was still a great deal to do when I got there in January 1963,« recalls Mezger. The camshafts moved above the cylinder heads to become ohc (overhead cams), plus the crankshaft now had eight bearings in order to improve vibration characteristics at high revs. The reason behind these complex measures was evident in the findings being made during the development of the eight-cylinder GP engine – there was no risk involved

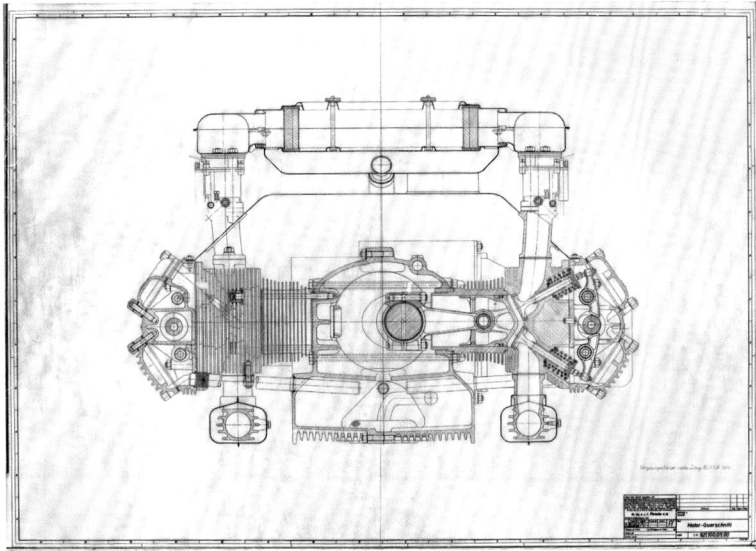

in trying out higher revs, because the crankshaft was better able to handle the greater forces inevitably arising from the higher engine speeds. The decision had been taken to go with a chain drive for the camshafts, and Mezger's main task at this point was to develop it.

The type 821 still had wet-sump lubrication. However, Ferdinand Piëch – who began his Porsche career on April 1, 1963 – took the decision to change the engine to dry-sump lubrication, which ensures an adequate oil supply to all engine components under the high centrifugal forces occurring in motorsport. Before coming to the view taken by the Development department as described by Ferdinand Piëch, we should, however, describe a detail of this design that would lead to unexpected complications just a few months later. Directly beneath the crankshaft was an intermediate shaft running at half the engine speed and driven by a helical gear pair. This intermediate shaft ran toward

the front and drove the oil pump, which was mounted on the front of the casing, directly behind the flywheel. Here, the pump generated the pressure used to force the oil through the engine's oil ducts. And it was precisely this intermediate shaft that would later stand in the way of another project.

But back to Ferdinand Piëch and his influence on the 901 engine, which was differentiated from the type 821 primarily by its dry-sump lubrication. He wrote in his *Auto.Biographie*, »In 1963 it still went without saying that Porsche in Stuttgart would hire a young engineer from the family – even if he did come from the wrong country. The desired separation of the spheres of influence exercised by Piëch/Austria and Porsche/Germany was somewhat permeable. That there were ultimately too many Piëchs and Porsches all together in Stuttgart is another story.

I began on April 1, 1963 working for the Race Engine Testing department. There were around a dozen of us, including engine designer Hans Mezger, who would later rise to fame and who, at the time, was second in charge of our department. It was a critical time, because the previous Porsche monoculture with the type 356 was facing replacement by the 911 (which was still

IN THE TYPE 821, THE TWO CRANKSHAFTS HAVE BEEN MOVED TO INSIDE THE CYLINDER HEADS –
AT THIS POINT, THE SIX-CYLINDER STILL HAS WET-SUMP LUBRICATION.

THERE
WAS
NOTHING
TO
IMPROVE
ON
THE 911

And this is exactly where my job began – despite the missed 904 deadline, we were still faced with having to develop the 911 engine as a racing motor in parallel with its development for series production. The target was 180 hp compared with the normal 130. The specifications laid down by my uncle included a Solex overflow carburetor. Instead of a floater, it had an overflow level, and depending on how fast you took the car round the bend, it could choke itself and come to a shuddering halt. As a member of the family, I was certainly able to take greater liberties than a normal staffer and ordered Weber triple downdraft carburetors instead. It let you drive left and right in faultless fashion without the engine strangling itself, and I soon had a reliable supply of 180 racing horses before the guys in series development managed to reach their 130 hp.

The upshot of this was that I was put in charge of the series-production engine, too. Throttling it down from 180 to 130 hp was not particularly difficult, but the wrong carburetor was still a problem. Professor Pierburg had a good way of dealing with my uncle, found reliable household staff for him, and was therefore able to retain favor for his carburetor. Deliveries of the 911 began in November 1964, but it was soon evident that things could not continue as they were and a switch was made to the Weber triple downdraft carb. I had already ensured the interchangeability of the two systems.«

Although the first cars were still built with the Solex triple carburetor, the Weber triple carburetor entered series production as of February 1966 starting with engine number 907001 and chassis number 305101. These changes meant that the engine was now equipped with all the systems necessary for a racing version – and it also fulfilled the power specifications laid down by Ferry Porsche – 130 hp at 6500 rpm.

called 901 at this point). The design was originated by my cousin Ferdinand Alexander Porsche – known as ›Butzi‹. With a head start on the 911, its motorsport derivative the 904 was also underway at the time – an exceptionally beautiful and progressive car with a glass-fiber reinforced plastic bodyshell. It was the very first car penned by my designer cousin, and he created it in one go, with virtually no further changes necessary. The plan was to max out the 911 engine straight away and try it in motorsport guise with the 904. It would then be scaled back into safer, more reliable territory for series-production use. The 904 bodyshell was finished, but the 911 six-cylinder not yet ready, meaning that we were unable to marry the two. That meant we had to pull the Fuhrmann four-cylinder back into service for the 904; the displacement was the same as for the unfinished six-cylinder – two liters.

FERRY PORSCHE AND HIS NEPHEW FERDINAND PIËCH CONTEMPLATE THE NEW 911 SIX-CYLINDER IN THE TESTING DEPARTMENT.

vertical-shaft variant with overhead camshafts developed by Ernst Fuhrmann. It was a complex motorsport technology that was too expensive for series-production use and that could only be repaired by specialists. Nobody could possibly know back then that the new design for the Porsche 911 would become the basis for countless motorsport variants that would win innumerable races worldwide.

The machine's motorsport career began as a modified series-production version that could be made lighter primarily through the use of different materials. The series-production geometry was retained except for the specifications for the valves, camshafts and channels. »We began developing the racing version in parallel in 1963, which was good for both engine variants,« recalls Mezger. But it was not finished in time. »The plan was to use the new six-cylinder in the Porsche 904. But the construction of the 100 units for homologation had to begin at the end of 1963 for there to be enough cars on the books by the start of 1964. So I reworked the Fuhrmann engine, as well.« Problems arose in the two-liter version with the con rod bearings and lubrication; there was shrinkage in the cam followers. And the shape of the camshafts was changed again in order to eke out more power. It was not until later that the new 911 engine also made its way into the Porsche 904. With a displacement of two liters, it produced 210 hp at 8000 rpm with carburetors. The use of a fuel injection system added a further 10 hp at the same engine speed. A one-off version with four overhead camshafts reached from 230 to 240 hp. In the Porsche 906, which was then offered with the six-cylinder only, it replaced the geriatric Fuhrmann engine once and for all.

Porsche Fahrer magazine also asked Hans Mezger whether its application as a motorsport engine was part of the original specification. These days, the engineer rather doubts that this was the case, saying, »That developed as work progressed.« However, this possibility marked a turning point in engine technology at Porsche. The pushrod engine of the Porsche 356 could never deny its derivation from the Beetle, and almost all of the racing versions used the

In designing the new engine, Mezger also brought with him crucial experience from his time in the

HANS METZGER WAS THE ENGINE SPECIALIST AT PORSCHE FOR DECADES.

088

WHILE THE TYPE 821 (ABOVE) STILL HAD WET-SUMP LUBRICATION,
THE 911 ENGINE (BELOW) WAS LAUNCHED WITH DRY-SUMP LUBRICATION.

THE POWER ROSE AND THE FUEL CONSUMPTION SANK

Formula 1 project, which impacted the design of the combustion chambers. »In designing the eight-cylinder engine for the Formula 1 project, we started with hemispherical combustion chambers and a valve angle of 90 degrees. Every time we narrowed the angle, two things happened – the power rose and the fuel consumption sank. This is an example of how experiences derived from motorsport are transferred into series production. I have always said that a good combustion chamber design doesn't cost anything.«

A great deal of time was spent at the drawing board working on the final valve arrangement. »We didn't have anything like a single-cylinder test engine for different heads. It was primarily a matter of gut instinct.« Ultimately, the intake valves had an angle of 27 degrees from the vertical, and the exhaust valves 33 degrees. Nothing was changed in this respect during the more than 30 years that the air-cooled 911 engine was used in its two-valve version says Mezger, »neither in the road-going nor the racing version.« The transmission was an all-new five-speed gearbox that was used for both the 904 Carrera GTS and the 901.

With this development, the new Porsche now had a suitable power unit that, on the one hand, remained true to the Porsche tradition while, on the other, being so well-prepared for the future that the engine continued to impress customers and motorsport enthusiasts in equal measure for many years to come. And if anyone had predicted to Ferry Porsche back then that this engine would still be used with enormous success on road and track decades later – albeit equipped with water cooling, but adapted for the most stringent of emissions legislation – he would probably have reaped just a smile of amazement in response.

WHILE THE SERIES-PRODUCTION ENGINE (PAGE 89, BELOW) WAS DELIVERED WITH 130 HP, THE SIX-CYLINDER IN THE 904 CARRERA GTS AND THE 911 R VARIANTS CAME WITH NO LESS THAN 210 HP.

TURBULENT DAYS AND LOTS OF TIMING ISSUES

THE STRESS MOUNTS

It is not easy to describe the genesis of a vehicle – too many things happen at the same time, in parallel. And let's not forget – this particular process took place in the late 1950s and early 1960s, when there were still no computers crunching their way through thousands of variations in a matter of hours and helping engineers reach their findings in double-quick time; it was a process that took weeks and months

THESE
WERE
TURBULENT
DAYS
AND
MONTHS

transmission. The people working on the interior were still struggling with colors and materials, while Marketing – still the Sales department in those days – explained to the engineers that customers expected better heating and rear side windows that could be popped open, and that the luggage compartment was too small anyway. It was problem after problem – a hectic search for fast detail solutions – new catastrophes every day – frenzied activity on the hour every hour.

And above everything else hung the great sword of Damocles that was the date of the car's first public appearance – in this case, September 12, 1963, a Thursday. This was the opening day of the 41st Frankfurt International Motor Show – and on this day, the 901 had to be finished.

back then. Or, to be more exact, thousands of variations were not even considered. Engineers depended instead on the benefit of experience and the knowledge and skills of employees. While the designers continued to fine-tune the details, the engineers and technical draftsmen hunched over their drawing boards and attempted to put the extremely complex technology where the Chief Engineer wanted it.

It was turbulent days and months that led up to September 12, because the design of the 901 did not progress as smoothly as the team in Zuffenhausen had expected. One of the reasons for this was the departure in the final development phase of Claus von Rücker, who left Porsche on April 1, 1962 to take up a new position with BMW in Munich. He was replaced by the 48 year-old Hans Tomala who had previously worked in tractor design and was given responsibility by Ferry Porsche for managing the factory, the Testing department and the Engineering office. Tomala was, as Ferdinand Piëch would later describe him, »certainly not a bad technician, but too stubborn to allow his ideas to be tested against the state-of-the-art.« This was an attitude that would lead to complications.

The first engine was finally being tested and, in the office next door, engineers held discussions with supply industry representatives on whether and how and when they could reckon on receiving the gears that might someday fulfill their purpose in the new

THE PROTOTYPE BEARING THE NUMBER 4 WAS DUBBED
»ZITRONENFALTER« (BRIMSTONE BUTTERFLY).

IN THE INITIAL PHASE, THE PROTOTYPES HAD ONLY TWO INSTRUMENT DIALS.

To begin with, however, the entire research and development program was checked, evaluated for its financial and technical feasibility and, where necessary, measures were taken. To start with, a wheelbase of 2100 millimeters was defined in 1961, whereby the fuel tank was located in front of the engine at the rear. A 1:7.5 clay model was built at the end of 1961 on this wheelbase, although it made the type 644 T8 look very squat and only offered space for two seats. Then it turned out that, in parallel, the chassis department had found a new front axle that not only saved space, but also offered sufficient room to locate the fuel tank above the front axle. This meant that – with a moderate extension of the wheelbase – there would now be enough interior space to find a 2+2 solution. Thus, the final decision was taken at the start of 1962 to work with a wheelbase of 221 centimeters. This was a decision that Ferry Porsche justified on the basis that, as a niche manufacturer, Porsche should not compete with the established manufacturers of full-size sedans.

No further fundamental changes were made to the successful shape demonstrated by Ferdinand Porsche junior with the T7 and T8 – it was simply a matter of adapting the lines to the now finally defined wheelbase. The front end received a few minor touch-ups, the windshield was set at a slightly steeper angle and the B-pillar tilted backward to ease the process of climbing into and out of the new car. Karl Ludvigsen described the wonderfully executed roofline in his excellent book *Porsche – Excellence was Expected* thus: »The roof line curved with absolute mastery and perfection from the windshield back to the trailing edge of the rear deck, which was punctured by a bold air-inlet grille that added visual interest to the coupe's rear view. As on the T-7, room was left between the widely spaced bumper guards for a license plate of any conceivable size or shape. In this practical, evolutionary way Ferry and Butzi Porsche arrived at the final contours of the car that would ultimately replace the 356.«

The interior was also closely oriented on the T7, although the dashboard that curved toward the driver was now equipped with five dials, with F. A. Porsche reserving the spot in the center for the rev counter. This finally put paid to the T7 solution with two large instrument dials. Although some of the early prototypes were still equipped with this solution, the twin-dial combo never made it into series production.

The design department under Erwin Komenda was initially responsible for engineering the chassis and bodyshell – and this is where the next set of difficulties arose, as Komenda's team had huge timing issues in designing the bodyshell. This was, of course, enormously unsettling to the management of Porsche and Reutter. It had all started with no particular frenzy, as initial discussions on a new project took place in early 1961 between Erwin Komenda and Walter Beierbach from Reutter. The content of one meeting was disclosed in the following letter dated April 10: »In the course of a conversation with our Mr. Komenda, you were broadly informed of bodyshell model programs for this year that will be apportioned to you. With this letter, we request that you complete styling models, hammer forms and prototypes of the type 764. We will furnish you with all the necessary drawing documentation in the course of the production process and, to a lesser degree, with fixtures and fittings made by suppliers. We herewith request that you build sufficient time for the type 764 program as described into your works schedule to the extent that it is practicable.«

What is irritating about this letter is the reference to the type 764, which otherwise appears in the Porsche archive in only one file from the second half of 1961. In this file, the type 764 includes drawings concerning »lights and headlamps«, »switches«, »wipers«, »instruments« and »engine, LM and AL« – and these drawings show only details; there is no associated correspondence. Dieter Landenberger, the Head of the Porsche Archive has the following to say on this particular mystery: »I assume that the type 764 was a styling variant that was not pursued further.«

A SCENE FROM THE DESIGN STUDIO – AT THE FRONT IS THE BLUE CLAY MODEL OF THE 754 T7, AT THE BACK IS AN EARLY 901.
NO-ONE KNOWS WHAT IS BENEATH THE WHITE TARPAULIN.

THERE IS
*NO MORE
ROOM LEFT*
IN THIS
SCHEDULE

WHETHER FERRY PORSCHE ACTUALLY EVER WORKED ON THE 901 PROTOTYPES IS UNKNOWN —
BUT HIS SON F. A. IS LOOKING ON VERY CLOSELY.

The discussions continued, the issue was firmed up and, on October 20, there is an exchange of correspondence complete with memo in which Reutter »states its agreement to take over responsibility for the design of a T8 bodyshell on the current T6 chassis.«

The document goes on to define pricing: »The bodyshell price cannot in any way exceed that of the current T6 bodyshell. The market even demands, if possible, a significant reduction in price through more rational production (tooling).« Further points were: »The new T8 bodyshell is to be built on the unchanged T6 chassis with platform number 644 T6. There is no requirement to allow for the installation of a Carrera engine. The exterior skin is to be constructed in line with the T7 prototype produced by Reutter. It should be taken into consideration that it must also be possible to build the vehicle as an open-top variant. In view of the short timescales involved (20 months), work must commence immediately. Reutter will first generate a program schedule working back from the final date (start-of-production July 1963). The tooling deadlines must be agreed as soon as possible with Karmann and other tooling suppliers as part of the program schedule.«

The extent to which the development costs for the new model were impacting the company's finances is evident in the sentence, »At the request of Porsche, Reutter has declared its willingness to consider the degree to which it can contribute to financing the costs in return for an increase in the price of the bodyshell.«

A subsequent meeting was set for November 7, 1961, for which coachbuilder Reutter sent the following letter to Dr. Ing. h.c. F. Porsche KG on November 3 as preparation for the appointment: »In line with our agreement, we have prepared a program schedule for the series-production development of a T8 bodyshell, which we include as an attachment.

We would not like to provide you with this raw program schedule without bringing to your attention the following points:

The feasibility of the program schedule is conditional upon:

- The starting points for the development of the construction in line with your requirements must be provided to us in full and without delay, in particular the design drawings for the T7 car on which the T8 bodyshell is to be based – if possible a model to a scale of around 1:10 and all details that you would wish to see realized by us in the design.
- The agreed upon assistance – if possible Mr. Schröder – must be made available to us as of Monday 13.11.1961. It has been agreed that a further designer will be made available to us for working out the details in the event that this appears necessary.
- Our tasks do not include: development of heating and ventilation, electrical equipment including lighting, the specification of instruments.
- For the development of the electrical equipment, which must be carried out in close coordination with our engineers, you have proposed to make available to us at the appropriate time 2 engineers as specialist consultants.

On the matter of the anticipated design costs and of the tooling costs, it is not possible to make any comment at this time. We will, however, return to you on these issues as soon as it becomes possible to assess the extent of the anticipated workload.

We would be very grateful if those points that remain open could be addressed as soon as possible and if we could be issued formally with an associated contract agreement. We consider it essential that you also afford us the necessary freedom in conducting this work. The deadlines incorporated in the program schedule are, as you can well imagine, the very shortest possible. There is no further room within these deadlines for unforeseen changes and hold-ups.

We extend our best regards in anticipation of your decision and contract issue in the very near future.«

Beierbach then appended the program schedule for the T8:

15.11.1961	Start of design
15. 1.1962	1st line plan for exterior
1. 3.1962	Hammer model for exterior skin
1. 3.1962	Start of build, 1st and 2nd prototype
15. 5.1962	1st prototype complete
15. 6.1962	2nd prototype complete
15. 6.1962	Start of master model, wood/epoxy resin
1. 8.1962	2nd line plan
1. 9.1962	End of master model, wood/epoxy resin
1. 9.1962	Final tooling sign-off for exterior skin
1.10.1962	Final tooling sign-off for inner skin
1.11.1962	Purchasing sign-off for accessories
1. 1.1963	Purchasing sign-off for raw materials
1. 3.1963	Equipment sign-off
1. 3.1963	Color sign-off
1. 6.1963	Production fixtures complete
10. 6.1963	Start of pilot run
1. 7.1963	End of pilot run
1. 8.1963	Start of production

The proposed timing plan was beyond ambitious – which makes it hardly surprising that a memo from November 7, 1961 included not only Messrs. Müller-Schöll and Beierbach from Reutter and Messrs. Porsche, Kern, Schmidt, Komenda, Klie and Tomala (all from Porsche), but also Messrs. Karmann, Krämer, Zobel and Rutsch, who were all part of the Karmann delegation. At this meeting, Karmann declared its willingness »to help in the production of tooling for the T8 through making available tooling capacity. Karmann proposes manufacturing the master model and the tooling for the exterior skin in Osnabrück, while the remaining tools would be made by Reutter or its suppliers.« The letter then goes on to allocate a few tasks and clarify the spheres of interest – »Reutter is of the opinion that it must manufacture the master model in wood and epoxy resin and that it would like to outsource parts of the exterior skin« – and then they agreed on further meetings.

The extent of the timing pressure is already apparent on November 17, 1961 in the letter addressed to the Reutter management team that – in reference

F. A. PORSCHE ALLEGEDLY DESIGNED SIX DIFFERENT AIR VENTS FOR THE REAR LID – THESE FOUR ARE DOCUMENTED.

to the discussions held between the management on October 20 and on November 7, 1961 – issued the substantial contract. »We hereby issue you with the contract for the design, including the detailing, of a Porsche bodyshell in the form as defined by us and based on our currently unchanged T6 chassis. The design shall be conducted in two versions – as a coupe and cabriolet – whereby for production reasons the underpinnings of both bodyshells shall be largely the same.

To progress the design work, we also make available to you for the duration of the design the services of our bodyshell design engineer Mr. Schröder and, as required on a case-by-case basis, those of a further detail design engineer. The design shall be carried out under your exclusive responsibility in accordance with our concept and in line with the program schedule issued by you in your letter dated 3.11.1961. Our engineering office is available to provide advice as and when required. In the event that changes to the platform are unavoidable, these will be carried out – in close coordination with your engineers – by our engineering office. The bodyshell to be designed is a Porsche bodyshell, the form of which remains our intellectual property.

The deadline of 1.8.1963 stated in your program schedule for the start of production of the coupé is considered binding, although we may be prepared to accept necessary alterations to individual deadlines between the start of design and start of production.

The deadline for start of production of the cabriolet was defined in a verbal agreement between your esteemed Mr. Beierbach and our Mr. W. Schmidt as 1.3.1964 at the latest. For reasons pertaining to the market, this deadline, too, may not be exceeded. It

VARIANT NUMBER 4 IS SEEN HERE MOUNTED ON PROTOTYPE NO. 4 – THE »ZITRONENFALTER«.

BY THE END OF 1962 THE TIMING PLAN WAS EXCEEDED BY NO LESS THAN FIVE MONTHS.

is our intention to commission you to produce the T8 bodyshells on T6 chassis as of July 1963, in volumes anticipated at around those of your current production. We will issue you with an associated contract for the purchase of tooling and preparations for production, including the design of jigs and fixtures, in due course.

We hereby confirm our agreement with your proposal that you invoice the first part of your design work in January 1962 against proof of completion. We are nevertheless interested in receiving from you as soon as possible a cost estimate for the total design program and for the tooling.

We extend our best regards in anticipation of a continued positive and fruitful cooperation …«

Stuttgart coachbuilder Reutter & Co. GmbH had started work at the end of 1961 on the design of the 901 and the preparations for its series production – but problems began to arise. Ferry Porsche had quickly turned to Wilhelm Karmann not least because of capacity bottlenecks at Reutter – where the groundwork for the 901 production was already underway. Karmann was still building the 356 C at this point, but there was plenty of capacity also to take on the construction of complete 901 bodyshells as of 1963. This was one of the main reasons that those in charge at Porsche, Karmann and Reutter met increasingly often in Zuffenhausen in order to reach agreement on progress being made in the preliminary work being carried out on the new project. Incidentally, it was after one of these many meetings, which had taken place on May 10, 1962, that the model designation 901 turned up in correspondence one week later – albeit initially enhanced with the T8 designation in brackets, just to make sure that all were clear on which model was being discussed. That Erwin Komenda and his team got into serious timing problems is now common knowledge and extensively documented in the relevant literature. Tobias Aichele put it as follows: »Following the meeting between Porsche, Karmann and Reutter, the Chief Engineer committed to submit a line plan on June 15 and to complete work on the underbody structure by June 30. Also in summer 1962, at a meeting between the management of Porsche and Reutter, Hans

Tomala stated that the design of the front axle and steering was now complete, meaning that framework construction around the front axle could commence. Because Erwin Komenda gave assurances that he would have completed the associated drawings, which were still outstanding, two weeks later (when there was still no delivery after four weeks, the tone sharpened considerably), Walter Beierbach committed on behalf of Reutter to have the bodyshell ready for the first drivable car by September 14. Time was now getting incredibly short. A close-to-production vehicle really should be available for testing before series production commences and before tooling is manufactured. It was not until a protocol dated June 28, 1963 that engineer Hans Hönick was able to write the first technical description because most of the technical components had finally been defined.«

If you compare these dates with the program schedule from November 7 the previous year, it is immediately apparent why the mood between those involved could not have been particularly good: Komenda had missed the timing plan by no less than five months, just for the delivery of the line plan – this meant that all the plans to put the 901 into production in parallel with its world premiere at the Frankfurt Motor Show were already a pipe dream.

Aside from the problems in delivering the documentation, the design was also turning out to be more complicated than initially thought, because Ferry Porsche's desire to use the 901 to replace the 356 entirely led persistently to debates of principle. One of the biggest debates arose from the question of the axle design on which to build the 901. More specifically, it was the front axle and its layout – not least because of time pressure – that caused the biggest arguments. Despite all

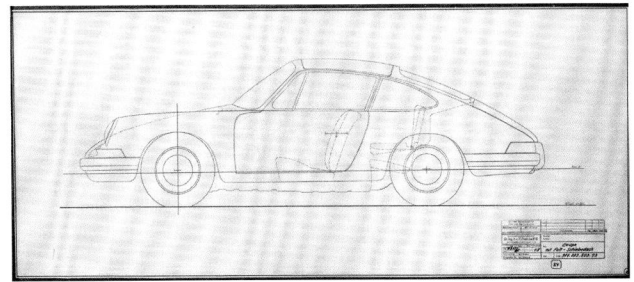

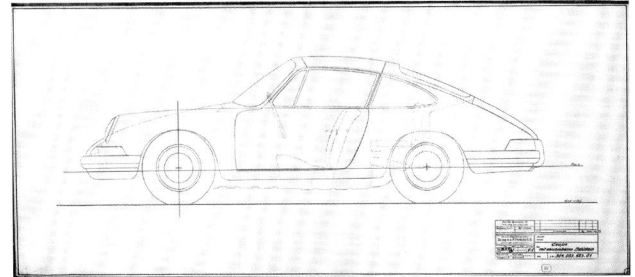

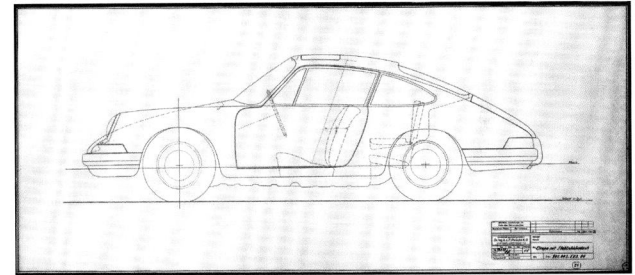

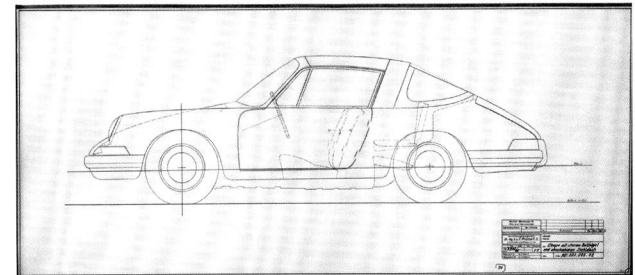

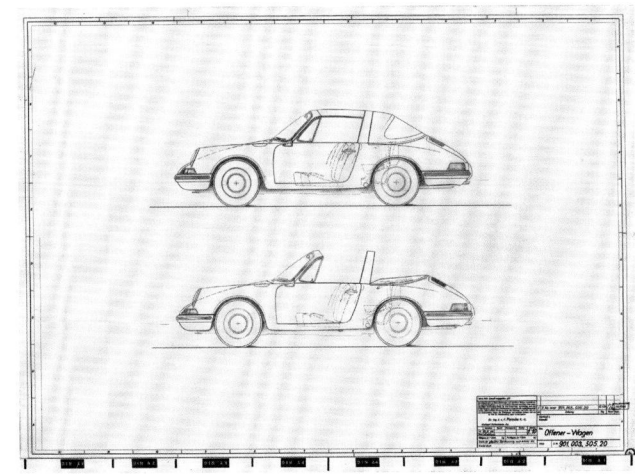

THEY CONSIDERED EVERY VARIANT – A COUPÉ WITH A FIXED AND REMOVABLE STEEL ROOF, A CANVAS SUNROOF, A TARGA AND AN OPEN-TOP VERSION.

THE PRIORITY
FOR THE
FRONT AXLE WAS
TO GAIN SPACE.

the complications, start of production of the new car still stood at July 1963. And, for this reason, Leopold Schmid – who was responsible for developing the engine and chassis – warned against a new design. It was clear to him that a new design could never be completed in the time available, which is why he made a case for an adaptation of the 356 front axle with more suspension travel. Ferry Porsche and Hans Tomala, on the other hand, wanted to take a new route here, too, and give the T8 a distinctly modern setup. Part of this plan was a new axle featuring a modified McPherson strut principle with a torsion bar suspension beneath it and a space-saving rack-and-pinion steering – both features that Helmuth Bott had also promoted at the beginning of 1962, albeit under the premise that there would be sufficient time available for the development, as it would not have been feasible to realize such a design by summer 1963.

Bott added that he had heard that the desired timeframe was no longer achievable anyway, »If, now that the bodyshell development is obviously taking longer than currently forecast, a start of production might be expected in 1964, the preference would be for a new chassis.« Just four days later, on January 15, 1962, an initial rough design for the new axle was ready, which was then – still against the will of Leopold Schmid – adopted with the rack-and-pinion steering. A decision described thus by Reinhard Seiffert in *Motor Revue*: »Despite the principle of not carrying over a Porsche feature without due critique, a great many Porsche features have been retained – drive layout, engine concept, form. But others have been left by the wayside, among them the suspension and the steering.«

The considerations that led to these changes are not complicated. The priority for the front axle was to gain space. Despite the front hood being pulled downward, the luggage space was supposed to increase, and that could only work if they got rid of the trailing-arm suspension with the transverse anti-roll bars. Lower wishbones and spring struts, i.e. a McPherson front suspension, offered the best solution. Further improvement came from giving the spring struts the function of the third attachment point and shock absorption only, while torsion bars located longitudinally beneath the car served for suspension. This sophisticated construction makes the front luggage compartment wider by those few centimeters occupied by the coil springs in normal suspension strut arrangements. The torsion bars were therefore not installed because a Porsche has to have torsion bars, but because they actually use up less space in this arrangement than any other suspension element.

It was possible to keep their transverse layout at the rear, although the previous swing axle was converted to a trailing-arm suspension. The reason for this was of a technical nature: In the interests of optimum handling characteristics, they wanted to avoid the toe-in and camber change that is a feature of swinging half-axles. The trailing arms (set at a slight angle) deliver very accurate wheel guidance. It was accepted that the added complication meant the wheels would have to be driven by double-jointed shafts.

The use of a different steering system also has plausible reasons. Rack-and-pinion steering requires little vertical space and thus does not impact

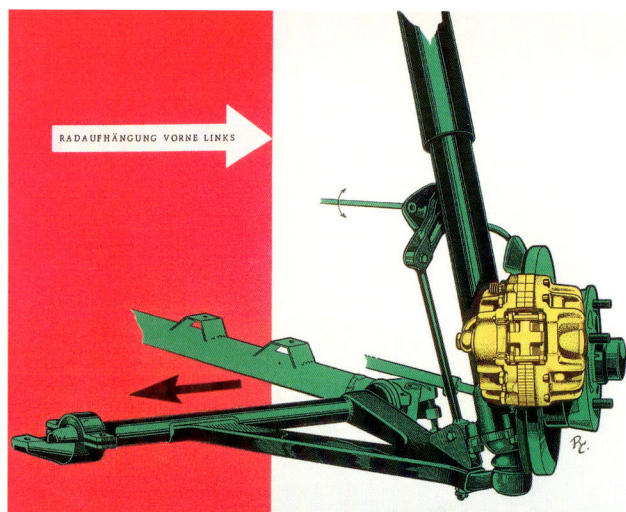

RADAUFHÄNGUNG VORNE LINKS

THE BEST SOLUTION FOR THE FRONT AXLE WAS LOWER WISHBONES WITH MCPHERSON STRUTS.

the front luggage compartment. The low-mounted steering box necessitates joints in the steering column that are considered highly desirable for another reason – they make the steering column less dangerous in the event of an accident. Porsche developed a telescopic steering column several years ago, but the current solution is without a doubt more straightforward and just as effective.«

Once again, it is evident that the development process was seen and described with hindsight as utterly stringent and unproblematic – which, in reality, was far from being the case, as indicated by an internal memo from Leopold F. Schmid to Erwin Komenda dated July 27, 1960. Schmid was an Austrian who had established himself as the designer of the Porsche synchronization. He wrote back then, »We have reason to assume that renowned firms will build collapsible steering columns in their passenger cars in the near future. The following are a few examples:

- It is known that DAIMLER-BENZ has been working since mid 1958 on the development of a collapsible and hydraulically damped steering column with a progressive damping effect.
- The TRIUMPH HERALD is already delivered as standard with a steering column that yields in the event of a collision.
- The AMERICAN MOTORS CORPORATION is interested in the collapsible and hydraulically damped steering column developed by PORSCHE.

We therefore intend to design the T7 chassis in such a way as to facilitate the installation of a collapsible steering column. The displacement path for the steering wheel is envisaged as being at least 65 mm, but not more than 85 mm. We ask that you take this into consideration in the design of the bodyshell.«

Thus, the idea of the telescopic steering column was born with the T7, but it took a long time for it to be accepted. Despite the words of warning, the people at Porsche were not particularly convinced by the benefits of this potentially life-saving technology, as indicated in a memo dated September 6, 1961:

»Mr. Komenda mentioned the difficulties he is having with the installation of the safety steering. Mr. Porsche was amazed that

A NEW
CHASSIS
WAS
CALLED
FOR
AT THE
START OF 1962

RADAUFHÄNGUNG HINTEN LINKS

AT THE REAR, A TRAILING-ARM SUSPENSION WITH A SHOCK ABSORBER REPLACED THE 356 SWING AXLE.

Verteiler:
Herrn Porsche
Herrn Porsche jr.
Herrn Tomala
Herrn Rombold
Herrn Reisspieß
Herrn Komenda
Herrn Linge
FV

A k t e n n o t i z
====================

Betr.: Erste Probefahrt mit Prototyp 901 am Freitag, 9.11.1962.

z.k. H.Kühn

A. Grundsätzliches

Sichtverhältnisse und Sitzposition sind gut.
Das Fahrzeug ist handlich und hat den Charakter des sportlichen
Wagens voll beibehalten. Die Fahreigenschaften entsprechen denen
unserer T 8 Vorläufer mit T 6 Karosse, d.h. das Fahrzeug übersteuert noch zu viel und spricht zu giftig am auf Lenkeinschläge,
in Wechselkurven noch nicht befriedigend. (Federabstimmung noch
nicht endgültig, fehlende neue Hinterachse).
Armaturen sind gut zu sehen, Sitze sind angenehm. Auf den Rücksitzen hat man nicht den Eindruck, besser untergebracht zu sein,
als im 356 B.
Stand- Brems- und Blinkleuchten sind gut sichtbar. Rückfahrschein-
werfer ergeben helles Licht und gute Streuung.

Vom Begleitfahrzeug aus wirkt das Fahrzeug von hinten fremd.
Man hat den Eindruck, als ob die Heckscheibe trapezförmig nach
hinten zusammenliefe. Das Fahrzeug wirkt zierlich und klein.

Gut ist auch die Abdeckung von Auspuff und Motor, wobei evtl. die
Begleiterscheinung, daß die Entdröhnpappe am Motorblech schon
nach der ersten kurzen Fahrt sehr weich wurde, mit der schlechteren
Kühlung des Topfes durch den Fahrtwind zusammenhängen mag.

B. Karosseriebeanstandungen

Türen klappern.
Fenster klappern.(Behelfsanordnung).
Handschuhkastendeckel springt auf.
Fahrzeug ist insgesamt laut (nicht Antidröhn gespritzt)
Scheiben beschlagen sehr stark (reicht für Winterbetrieb Düsenquer-
schnitt aus?).
Motorraumbeleuchtung leuchtet durch Deckelkissen (andere Anbringung
möglich?).
Warum kein symmetrischer Schlüssel für Tür- und Lenkschloß?

C. Fahrgestellbeanstandungen

Lenkung ist vor allem in Mittelstellung zäh und träge, trotzdem
bei Korrekturen giftig, hat in Mittelstellung etwas Spiel.
Fahrzeug übersteuert wie Wagen 109.
Heizung stinkt.
Getriebe heult.
Vorderachse falsch eingestellt, Fahrzeug hat zu wenig Bodenfreiheit.
Querremnfugen kommen durch, als ob Gummipuffer anstünden.
Vorderachse schlägt durch.
Lenkrad sitzt nicht in Mittelstellung.
Drehzahlmesser zeigt wahrscheinlich zu viel an.
Bremse hat starke Pedalwegänderungen. Nach einigen km Fahrt ohne
Bremsung ist man am Bodenbrett. Durch Pumpen kommt das Pedal wieder
zurück.

- 2 -

- 2 -

D. Sonstiges

Licht gut, Schaltung gut.
V_{max} Tunnel bei Behinderung 20,8 - 173 km/h. Anzeige Drehzahlmesser
6100 U/min.

E. Montageprogramm für 12. und 13.10.62.

Lenkradstellung berichtigen.
Handschuhkastendeckel-Befestigung ändern.
Bodenbrett für Beifahrer anbringen.
Abstand Auspufftopf - Motorblech kontrollieren (Temperatur!).
Drehzahlmesser eichen.
Getriebe ausbauen und Tachometerantrieb einbauen.
Wenn Drehzahlmesser nicht korrigiert werden kann, zusätzlicher
Einbau Hartmann & Braun-Gerät.
Raderhebungen aufnehmen, Rahmenelastizität- und Lenkelastizität
messen.
Vorderachse richtigstellen.
Handbremse einbauen.
Bremse entlüften und untersuchen.

Stgt.-Zuffenhausen, 12.11.1962
FV/Bo-scho

(Bott)

anybody would want such a thing. If the item becomes too expensive, it will simply not be used.« Thus, it would take a few more months for this feature to find acceptance, and for those involved finally to be clear on how the 901 should now be equipped and positioned.

And it would take until June 28 for engineer Hans Hönick finally to be able to write the first exact technical description of the new type 901 – a time by which they had actually wanted already to be driving the second prototype around the test track. With delays of this magnitude, it can come as no surprise that every department at Porsche, as well as Reutter and Karmann, was at work day and night. These extra shifts may well have alleviated the time problem, but they caused the development costs to sky-rocket even further, putting increasing stress on Ferry Porsche. Nevertheless, this speed meant that Karmann managed, on November 15, 1962, to complete the first two master models. These were signed off in Osnabrück by F. A. Porsche, Tomala, Albrecht, Beierbach – to name just a few. At the request of F. A. Porsche, they were painted black and polished. The planned deadlines of September 1, 1962 may have been missed by two and a half months, but at least the overrun had been reduced to some degree.

Tobias Aichele wrote about the events of November 15, 1962. »F. A. Porsche had asked that the black master models be presented in a well-lit space and not placed on a podium. Although the Porsche representatives were generally satisfied with the quality, some details still had to be reworked – the door handle cavity, the joint between the fender and the dashboard cowl, the rear lid and the rear bumper, the front bumper and the indents for the windshield wipers in the dashboard cowl. Two weeks were agreed for carrying out the rectifications.

In the meantime, Porsche engineer Robert Binder had also completed the first fully relevant design drawing

THE *DEADLINE*
OVERRUN
COULD
FINALLY
BE SOMEWHAT
REDUCED

with the drawing number 901.003.501.00. At the time, drawings were always done in 1:10 scale.«

However, November 1962 was not the most important month just for form and design. It was around this time – November 9, 1962 to be precise – that the first prototype 901 was also completed, with a platform built by Porsche and a bodyshell built by Reutter. Its color was white and its nickname was »Petrel«. This marked the start of the months in which the new baby had to learn to walk – it still was not clear whether the 901 would be able to fulfill all the wishes of its parents. But Helmuth Bott, who was the first engineer to sit behind the wheel of »Petrel«, was confident, »The vehicle handles well and has fully retained the character of a sporty car.«

ONLY ENGINEERS CAN DESCRIBE THE MAIDEN DRIVE OF A NEW PORSCHE SPORTS CAR SO CLINICALLY AND FACTUALLY.

THE
901 FINALLY
MAKES IT
TO THE
ROAD

&

THE
COMPANY
BREATHES
A SIGH
OF RELIEF

Far later than expected, the 901 finally made it to the road at the end of 1962 – the test drives with the first prototype began in the late evening of November 9, 1962 and at the wheel once again was Helmuth Bott, who in the meantime had been promoted to Head of Test Driving. And although Bott had plenty of detail complaints – »Doors rattle. Windows rattle. Heating stinks. Transmission howls. Steering is sticky and sluggish, especially in the middle position, but tenacious under correction, with some play in the middle position« – the man who would later become the Board Member for Technical Development did not seem dissatisfied, also remarking, »Safety characteristics and seating position are good. The vehicle handles well and has fully retained the character of a sporty car. Instruments are clearly visible, seats are comfortable.«

THIS WAS THE MOMENT EAGERLY AWAITED FOR YEARS – THE 901 WAS FINALLY ON SHOW TO THE PUBLIC.

Verteiler:
Herrn Porsche
Herrn Porsche jr.
Herrn Tomala
Herrn Rombold
Herrn Reimspieß/
Herrn Hönick
Herrn Komenda
Herrn Linge
FV

A k t e n n o t i z

Betr.: Zweite Probefahrt mit Prototyp 901 am
Mittwoch, 14.11.1962

Außentemperatur + 6° C, Straßen trocken.
Meßfahrten zwischen 21.00 und 22.00 Uhr, windstill.

Meßwerte:

Stehender km in 2 Richtungen gefahren: im Mittel - 35,3, 34.7
mittlere Geschwindigkeit 104 km/h. (Anfahrvorgang nicht ganz korrekt,
da Kupplung rupft).

Höchstgeschwindigkeit am Tunnel - 188 km/h bei Bremsleistung des
Motors 88,7 PS.

Bei Drehzahl 6100 abfallend auf 6000 nach Drehzahlmesser (Eichkurve
liegt im Augenblick noch nicht vor).
Tachoanzeige bei dieser Geschwindigkeit 197 km/h, Voreilung 5 %.

Tachoanzeige bei 60 km/h = 60 km/h
bei 120 km/h = 120 km/h
Abweichung also nur im oberen Bereich.

Lenkung:

Schon bei der Ausfahrt war die Lenkung nicht so lebendig wie unsere
Serienlenkung. Während der Fahrt wurde sie immer schwergängiger und
nach ca. 50 km mußte sie selbst bei engen Kurven in die 0-Lage zurück-
gezogen werden.

Bremsen:

Die eingebaute Girling-Bremse mit Girling-Hauptbremszylinder ist an-
genehm im Fußdruck, gut in der Bremswirkung und verzieht nicht aus hoher
Geschwindigkeit. Der Pedalweg wechselt immer noch stark.
Bei einer Vollbremsung aus 205 km/h war das Bremspedal am Bodenbrett.
Nach 5 Bremsungen aus 140 km/h bis nahezu Stillstand wurde ein starkes
Geräusch durch schleifende Bremsbacken an der Scheibe hörbar, das sich
im Verlauf von etwa 2 km wieder vollständig verlor. Außerdem qualmte
und stank die Bremse sehr stark bei den letzten beiden Bremsungen.

Drehzahlmesser:

Das Instrument funktionierte am Anfang sehr gut. Die Nadel stand ruhig
und eilte nicht merklich vor. Nach ca. 20 km Fahrt sprang die Nadel
plötzlich auf 0 zurück und setzte von Zeit zu Zeit stark zappelnd wieder
ein (Gerät nicht in Ordnung).

Motor:

Der eingebaute Motor hatte einen sehr schlechten Leerlauf (pendelnd von
800 auf 100 U/min). Starke Vibrationen werden im Leerlauf auf den Wagen
übertragen. Im Gegensatz zu guten Serienmotoren fiel die Drehzahl bei
leichten Steigungen stark zurück. Die Probefahrt wurde unterbrochen, da die
Lenkung so stark klebte, daß das Fahrzeug nicht mehr betriebssicher war.

- 2 -

- 2 -

Weiteres Montageprogramm

1.) Motor ausbauen und an FV übergeben.
2.) Kupplung nachsehen (rupft stark).
3.) Motor-Getriebe-Aufhängung Shore-Härte prüfen
(Kupplungsrupfen, starke Geräuschübertragung).
4.) Bremsen überprüfen.
Bei Vollbremsung blockierten die beiden linken Räder.
Von den rechten Rädern zeichnet sich keine Bremsspur ab.
Bremspedal schlägt hart an beim Zurückschnalzen.
5.) Drehzahlmesser Gerät ausbauen, überprüfen.
Eichkurve am Armaturenbrett ankleben.
6.) Spurstangen umhängen, Reibung Lenkgetriebe und Lenkungsdämpfer
feststellen. Bei zu großer Reibung in Lenkgetriebe Lenkgetriebe
demontieren und Spezialfett einfüllen.
7.) Außenspiegel montieren nach Angaben der Abteilung Studio.
8.) Haltegriff für Beifahrer nach Anweisung Studio anbringen.
9.) Fahrzeug vermessen, Lenkradstellung korrigieren.
10.) Bedienung von Scheibenwischer und -wascher angenehm, Lenkschloß jedoch sehr schlecht zugänglich, unmöglich.
11.) Rahmenelastizitäts- und Lenkelastizitätsmessungen für Samstag
vorbereiten.

Nächste Probefahrt voraussichtlich Montag, den 21.11.1962.

x) Handbremse in der Wirkung ausreichend nur bei sehr starkem Anziehen
des Handbremshebels (für eine Frau nicht mehr zumutbar).

Stgt.-Zuffenhausen, 15.11.1962
FV/Bo-scho

(Bott)

A k t e n n o t i z

Verteiler:
Herrn Porsche
Herrn Porsche jr.
Herrn Tomala
Herrn Rombold
Herrn Reimspieß/
Herrn Hönick
Herrn Komenda
Herrn Linge
MV
FV

Betr.: 3. Probefahrt mit Prototyp 901 am Dienstag,
27.11.1962

Außentemperatur + 1° C, fast windstill.

Teilnehmer: die Herren Rombold, Spannagel, Bott.

Grundsätzliches:

Karosse

Fußauflage für Beifahrer sollte flacher sein.
Ausstellfenster verursacht starkes Windgeräusch.
Bedienung des Ausstellfensters schlecht, da gerändelte Scheibe nicht
griffig genug.
Scheibe hat in jeder Öffnungsstellung zu viel Spiel.
Scheibe hat in jeder Öffnungsstellung zu viele Umdrehungen notwendig, Scheibe klemmt.
Türheber geht schwer, zu schwach.
Handschuhkastenarretierung sehr gut, am Beifahrersitz zu weit hinten.
Armlehne am Fahrersitz sehr gut.
Beide Armlehnen lose.
Rücklehnenverstellung schlecht zu bedienen, liegt am Schweller an.
Kopfraum und Knieraum auf Rücksitzen erscheinen geringer als am
Serienfahrzeug.
Zündschloß sehr schlecht zu erreichen, siehe Versuchsbericht E 1055.
Heizbetätigung sitzt zu weit vorne und sollte durch einfachen Hebel
ersetzt werden.
Zahlen der Instrumente zu kontrastarm. Schlechte Ablesemöglichkeit auch
bei max. Einstellung.
Ablage hinter den Rücksitzen sollte zweckmäßigerweise entweder
horizontal sein oder eine Haltekante bekommen.
Lehnen der Rücksitze müssen eine Arretierungsmöglichkeit erhalten, an
Handbremshebel sitzt zu weit vorne.
Die beiden Sonnenblenden haben an den Außenseiten Metallbügel, an
welchen man sich beim Unfall verletzen kann.

Allgemeine Beanstandungen:

Zwischen Lenkrad und Lenkgetriebe streift etwas in Höhe der Mittel-
stellung.
Rechte Türe scheppert.
Starke Zugluft durch Zigarrenanzünderloch.
Abblendlicht zu kurz.
Abblendlicht, Wege dürften kleiner sein.
Schaltung gut, Wege dürften kleiner sein als im Serienfahrzeug.
Starker Abgasgeruch im Schub, intensiver als im Serienfahrzeug.
Heizleistung gut.
Motordeckel scheppert. Kofferraumbeleuchtung funktioniert nicht.
Ascher fehlt. Handgriff für Beifahrer fehlt.
Für den Benzintank sollte ein Unterschutz vorgesehen werden.
Bremse hat nach wie vor starke Pedalwegänderungen.

Stgt.-Zuffenhausen, 28.11.1962
FV/Bo-scho

(Bott)

IT TOOK
A LONG
TIME FOR
THE
QUALITY
TO BE
RIGHT

speed of 205 km/h was recorded – not bad for a sports car on its second outing. The third test drive was scheduled for the end of November and the early problems were gradually addressed – even though there were still plenty of improvements to be made on the bodyshell, with regular complaints of loud wind noise and too much play in the windows.

The weaknesses were systematically eliminated in the course of the many thousands of kilometers that the prototypes covered over the months and years that followed – but it took a long time for the 901 to reach a standard of quality worthy of the Porsche name. The test drivers had a series of issues to address while on the road, they had to weld axles, work on the electrics, conduct emergency repairs or even have the vehicle brought back to the workshop on a trailer. No wonder that those responsible in Zuffenhausen became restless over the months that followed. There was an endless series of test reports, and crisis meetings were called virtually on a daily basis, at which piles of complaints were collected and forwarded to the respective departments for the problems to be addressed and solved. There was a continuous stream of memos that now fill a long series of files. And, of those, just one is shown here as a typical example.

The assembly complaints on car 901/9 filled no less than two closely printed pages on July 8, 1964. They arose during the assembly of the vehicle in the period from June 11 to July 6:

• Transmission touching bodyshell rear right. Body beaten out to accommodate.

The second test drive took place just five days later – again in the evening, between 9 and 10pm. The temperature stood at 6 degrees Celsius and there was no wind. It was on this evening that the 901 completed its first standing kilometer in two directions. The time for that was 34.7 seconds, at an average speed of 104 km/h. Bott noted that initial acceleration was not quite right, that the clutch was juddering. And an initial top

- Rear dampers left and right touching bodyshell from lower edge to center of tulip cavities; tulip cavities were beaten out to accommodate.
- Tank installation poor. Stiffening panel for rear tank cutout at around steering height had to be flanged in order to mount the tank with filter connectors for engine and heating.
- Lower edge of fuel-tank sender touching tank floor radius; attachment flange had to be turned.
- Screw holes for tank attachment are covered by tank. Tank had to be sanded down in those places.
- Seal between tank and bodyshell too thick.
- Filter connector on tank requires revision. Delrin crown nut does not provide sufficient compression to seal with the hard aluminum seal ring. Filter connector was revised and assembled without aluminum seal ring.
- Bore for gasoline line for Webasto heating unit not in accordance with drawing.
- Bore for cable to brake light switch had to be drilled around 10 mm higher. Blocked by brake line.
- Steering coupling runs against bodyshell. Had to be cut out.
- Aperture for steering-column tube through dashboard and trunk not flush; had to be reworked.
- Chamfer for main brake cylinder mounting flange had to be reworked.
- Free space between toothed segment and locking lever measures just 0.2 mm when handbrake off.
- Pushrod for handbrake lever jumps out when brake is over-tensioned. Pushrod secured with pins.
- Yoke for handbrake rocker too strong or bolt too short. Bolt circlip sticks and does not sit cleanly in the groove.
- Rear brake discs left and right rub on brake shoe stop.
- Brake light switch had to be turned into connector in vice in order to seal. Thread probably insufficiently conical.
- Front axle cover panel rubs on steering damper mount.
- Rear axle shafts rub on control arms.
- Throttle control linkage rubs on handbrake tube in tunnel and on tunnel brace.
- Clutch pedal backstop cannot be adjusted once installed.
- Gas pedal backstop too low.
- Driver-side floor panel had to be reworked at clutch and brake recesses.
- Exhaust touches skirt and bumper guards; exhaust pipe touches bodyshell.
- Oil suction pipe too long; oil return pipe too short.
- Seam and bracket added to engine paneling front right for fixing oil return pipe.
- Exhaust aperture in the bodyshell for Webasto heating had to be reworked.
- Wiper assembly is hard to install. Motor and connecting rods have to be installed and removed one by one.
- Changing the instruments and switches and installing the radio is very difficult without removing the wiper assembly.
- Holes for heating switches, fog lamps and hazard light had to be reworked.
- Sensor for oil level display pushes against filter, meaning incomplete travel on read-out.
- Steering lock installation not possible without beating out the bodyshell first.

That was quite a list – and memos of this kind exist in vast quantities. All of this made those involved increasingly nervous, while the number of nightshifts and extra shifts mounted. In fact, the new car had so many details that were not yet thought through that even the car that Ferry Porsche received in fall 1964 – one year after the presentation in Frankfurt – shocked Helmuth Bott when he first drove it. Bott wrote in his report on the vehicle with the chassis number 300003

IN PARALLEL TO THE DEVELOPMENT COSTS, PORSCHE HAD ALSO SPENT A GREAT DEAL OF MONEY ON
THE RESEARCH CENTER IN WEISSACH, WHERE THE NEW CAR WAS UNDERGOING EXTENSIVE TESTING
COACHBUILDERS REUTTER ALSO HAD TO BE ACQUIRED AND PAID FOR IN JULY 1963.

A k t e n n o t i z
====================

Betr.: Erste Probefahrt mit Fahrzeug 901/3, Fg.Nr. 300 003
       (Wagen von Herrn Porsche)
_____

Motor: In kaltem Zustand kein Leerlauf, Leerlauf warm
                bei 1500 U/min, Übergangslöcher in kaltem Zustand.
                Motorleistung gut, Motorgeräusch wie Wagen 901/8
                und 901/9. Motorheizung sehr heiß, stellt nicht
                ganz ab. Gaspedal zäh, geht langsam zurück.

Kupplung: Kurzer Pedalweg, löst knapp aus.

Getriebe: Schubrasseln im 3. Gang stärker als Wagen 901/8
                und 901/9, sonst Getriebegeräusche wie bekannt.
                Schaltung zäh und schwergängig.

Bremse: Bremswirkung nach kurzem Einbremsen gut, starke
                Pedalwegänderung.

Vorderachse: Starkes Lenkungsvibrieren in jedem Geschwindig-
                keitsbereich.

Hinterachse: Vibrationen bei Geschwindigkeiten über 140 km/h.

Fahreigen-   Fahrzeug noch etwas zäh und bockig, Geradeauslauf-
schaften: eigenschaften unbefriedigend, übersteuert beim
                Kurvenfahren, starke Reaktion auf Gaswechsel.

Karosse: Fensterkurbeln gehen zu schwer,
                Türfensterflattern,
                Windgeräusch ab 80 km/h,
                Klappergeräusch hinten rechts und linke Türe,
                Rechter Fensterrahmen liegt bei geschlossener Türe
                nicht an und hebt bei 180 km/h um mindestens 10 mm
                ab.
                Sitz zu hoch.

Stgt.-Zuffenhausen, 18.9.1964   *Bott*
VF/Bo-kf   (Bott)

*gaz kabel
motor*

THE DIFFICULTIES OF PRODUCTION START-UP ARE EVIDENT IN THE REPORT ON THE FIRST TEST DRIVE OF FERRY PORSCHE'S CAR —
TWO MONTHS BEFORE DELIVERY OF THE FIRST CUSTOMER VEHICLES.

»VEHICLE
STILL
RATHER
HEAVY-GOING
AND
UNRULY«

on September 18: »No idling when cold. Transition holes when cold. Engine heating very hot, does not switch off completely. Gas pedal stiff, travel very slow. Gearshift sticky and heavy. Heavy steering vibration at all speeds. Directional stability unsatisfactory, oversteers in corners, strong charge-cycle reactions.« And still there was wind noise – and the window frames still did not sit right, lifting from the bodyshell at high speeds.

However, there were also positive signs. The long-distance vehicles came home more frequently without major problems – and the tone of the engineers softened – as Herbert Linge wrote after a 4782-kilometer training drive on the Tour de France (an extremely popular endurance race through France at the time) with car 901/8, »Overall, the engine leaves an outstanding impression. Performance from 2500 to 7000 rpm very good and free-revving. Because the engine is very quiet inside the vehicle you have to make sure you don't over-rev it (warning light at 6800 rpm?)« He goes on, »Vehicle very comfortable and can also be driven very fast without straining itself.« There is, of course, also criticism, »Clutch action is too heavy; after a long time on the road, it is no longer possible to achieve a clean declutch, which causes the gears to crash and overstresses the synchronization. The rear wheels tramp on poor road surfaces and would require slightly heavier damping.« And then, of course, comes the obligatory criticism, »Windows whistle a great

deal at higher speeds when closed. They rattle when slightly open. Window winding mechanism too heavy.« And we also know today that the first 911s delivered were brought to series maturity in no small part by customers – loyal customers who were happy to accept the factory's admittedly very accommodating attitude in order to make their contribution as part of the Porsche family to the perfection of this fascinating vehicle.

Herbert Linge still recalls visits to Porsche owners across the world, whom he was able to help by resetting the carburetor or addressing other weaknesses, »One of the first 911 customers used the car in Paris city traffic. And because the spark plugs regularly sooted up, I drove it one day on the nearby highway heading toward Versailles and revved the engine up to the rev limiter. After a short time, the six-cylinder was running A1 and the 911 was as it should be. I then advised the owner to put the pedal to the metal once a week on the highway – which he of course did with pleasure.« Once more, customers demonstrated that they were prepared to play their part in perfecting a new Porsche – when they felt suitably supported by the factory.

While the engineers and technicians ran up their kilometers on the test stands, on the back roads and on the autobahns, the test facility on the new Porsche test site in Weissach gradually came on stream. Herbert Linge, who was born in Weissach, bought a large site in January 1960 – just 25 km away from the main factory in Zuffenhausen – for constructing a test facility. The stony area was extensively overgrown and apparently worthless for agriculture. Many plots of land had not been cultivated for years. Ground was broken on October 16, 1961. Exactly

»VEHICLE VERY COMFORTABLE AND CAN ALSO BE DRIVEN VERY FAST WITHOUT STRAINING ITSELF.«

TEST DRIVERS LOVE TO DRIVE ON SNOW – A FORM OF PROPULSION THAT PROTOTYPE NUMBER 4 WAS ALSO ABLE TO EXPERIENCE.

one year later, the first phase was completed – a test drive station with skid pan (circular track) and a number of different roads. And on May 30, 1963, the site was completely up and running. Later, on March 8, 1966, Porsche announced that it planned to move the entire development function to Weissach – a decision that was also very quickly implemented. Thus, on July 1, 1971, the Entwicklungszentrum Weissach (EZW) (Weissach Development Center) entered partial service. Today, Weissach is one of the world's most important test and design centers. And Weissach played a major role in the development of the 901 – this is where the car received its very last fine tuning.

By early 1963, it was also clear to those in charge that the 901 would be considerably more expensive than the 356 SC – development costs were ballooning out of control and it was also patently obvious in Zuffenhausen that, although Karmann delivered very good quality, it came at a price. Plus, a cost proposal had also been submitted by Weinsberg coachbuilders for parts of the production facilities that was around 40 percent below the Reutter proposal. This meant that one more partner now had to be taken into consideration in the planning and coordination process. After Ferry Porsche had continually stated that the matter of cost reduction was of the very highest priority – »Please ensure that the price of a 901 body remains below that of a 356 body« – the calculation ended up being something quite different altogether. In a letter to Reutter on November 8, 1963, Porsche thus signed off on the following pricing:

Body No.	1	–	100	unit price	DM 6000
Body No.	101	–	200	unit price	DM 5400
Body No.	201	–	500	unit price	DM 4800
Body No.	501	–	1000	unit price	DM 4000

Added to that were the significantly more expensive engine, a brake system adapted to suit the increased performance, new running gear complete with new steering, better lighting units, more premium materials, etc. etc. – plus, the 901 also had to be adapted to meet the increasing expectations of an ever more demanding audience. Porsche also had to pay for the development costs of the 901 (estimated at around 15 million Deutschmarks) the impending more-or-less voluntary takeover of the Reutter coachworks in July 1963, as well as the considerable investments in Weissach. To put it bluntly, Dr. Ing. h.c. F. Porsche KG was bitterly dependent upon the success of the 901 – otherwise the future of the company would have been in serious trouble.

How uncertain the Sales department was about pricing is also evident in the various different sums that were called up at various different times. At the Frankfurt Motor Show in 1963, the car was priced at 23 900 Marks. In December 1963, an internal memo appeared stating that three versions of the 901

PROTOTYPE NUMBER 2 – KNOWN AS »THE BAT« – WAS PREPARED WITH SCREWED-ON CLADDING FOR POSED PRESS SHOTS.

THE 356 WAS LOWER AND WIDER THAN THE 901 – YET THE 901 SEEMED MORE MATURE AND REFINED.

ALTHOUGH 901 AND 356 BOTH HAD THE TYPICAL PORSCHE SILHOUETTE, THE 901 WAS CONSIDERABLY LARGER.

A PROUD TEAM CELEBRATES THE 904 CARRERA GTS AND THE NEW 901 — AND FERRY PORSCHE SITS FRONT AND CENTER.

should now be offered. A 901 de Luxe with all-leather upholstery for 22 400 Marks; a standard version with four cylinders, artificial leather and a wooden steering wheel for 17 500 Marks (this should later become the 912) and a 901 S that, with 150 instead of the regular 130 hp, should be sold for 23 900 Marks – a price that was still under discussion for the 130 hp version in September. In the end, it took until the 1967 model year for a 911 S version to appear, which then delivered 160 hp.

What makes the matter somewhat more complicated is the price of 23 700 Marks that was stated in fall 1964 by *Motor Revue* – and bearing in mind the good relationship between the publishing house and the factory, this had surely been agreed. In parallel, the price tag on the 356 C 1600 was 14 950 Marks, while the 356 SC Coupe was listed at 16 450 Marks. Just as expensive as the 901 was the Carrera 2 Coupe with the complicated Fuhrmann dual-camshaft engine – only the 904 Carrera GTS cost more at 29 700 Marks.

That was a big price increase for many loyal 356 customers – the difference of 8750 Marks between the 356 C Coupe and the 901 was almost enough to buy a Mercedes-Benz 190 sedan or enough for a Karmann Ghia Coupe (6935 Marks) plus the first two-year's worth of gas. As it turned out, the price was dropped to 22 900 Marks within a year – but these 800 Marks did not make much of a difference. Porsche suddenly found itself in direct competition with exotic and sporty alternatives like the Alfa Romeo 2600 Sprint, the sporty Jaguar sedans, the Lancia Flaminia Coupe – even the new, elegant Mercedes-Benz 230 SL was more than 2000 Marks cheaper.

The apparently enthusiastic first-drive reports were only of limited help – but Porsche was prepared for this and had considered at a relatively early stage how they could offer a less expensive sibling alongside the 901. It would have less power – but at a time when the VW Beetle with a top speed of 115 km/h was Germany's most popular car, 180 or 190 km/h would still be accepted as extremely sporty. Paul Hensler, later Chief Departmental Manager for Development, Mechanics, was therefore tasked with developing a four-cylinder from the six-cylinder. By sharing many of its parts with the larger unit, it should be cost-effective to produce. This engine would also have had the benefit of not being rooted in the old VW engine, but in a genuine Porsche development.

»But the job could not be completed, because reducing the engine by two cylinders of 333 ccm each left it with a displacement of just 1334 ccm, which was definitely too small. We really wanted to offer a displacement of at least 1.6 liters,« recalls Paul Hensler. »And when we were looking for options that would provide a suitable increase in engine size, we hit up against two new problems. Firstly, we had adopted – after a suitable testing program – a technology for the individual cylinders that would be introduced in the four-cylinder shortly before the end of the 356 SC production, and then used from the outset in the 901. They were *Biral* cylinders, which had bearing surfaces made from high-quality cast iron encased in pressure-cast aluminum with cooling ribs for heat dissipation. The wafer-thin cast-iron surfaces meant that a substantial increase in the bore size would be out of the question – otherwise the aluminum pistons and their steel rings would have run directly on the pressure-cast aluminum casing. We were able to increase the bore to 84 mm for the 1970 model year, taking the engines up from 1991 cm^3 to 2195 cm^3. But any more simply was not possible. However, the increase in bore size to 84 mm would have brought the planned four-cylinder up to just 1463 cm^3.

And, while we were thinking about increasing the stroke, we had to take into account that the intermediate shaft driving the oil pumps for the dry-sump lubrication, as well as the bottom-mounted oil pump package, were mounted so closely beneath the crankshaft that any attempt at an increase would have resulted in the shaft hitting the oil pumps. And, because the tooling contract had already been issued for the casting that held the crankshaft, there was absolutely no question of making the design changes that would have been necessary – this shortcoming was not addressed with a suitable new design until the 2.7-liter engine.« But, with typical Swabian attention to detail, Hans Mezger nevertheless put together a cost comparison for

PORSCHE HAD NO OPTION – THEY HAD TO TURN BACK TO THE 356 ENGINE.

the different engines and sent it to Ferry Porsche in the internal mail. And we can derive from it that the net costs for the type 901 six-cylinder engine, including assembly, were 2702 Marks; while the four-cylinder engine – based on the type 901 – would have cost 2035 Marks. By way of comparison, the two-liter, four-cylinder engine with push rods was calculated at ca. 1800 Marks.

So Porsche was left with no choice but to fall back on the proven four-cylinder from the 356 SC for the 902 – as the car was called in the initial documentation. While the necessary modifications had resulted in its output of 90 hp being more than five hp less than in the 356 SC, it had quieter and more cultivated running characteristics, largely as the result of larger air filters. Ferdinand Piëch wrote in his *Auto.Biographie* on this topic, »A sad problem for the company during this time was the unstable sales figures for the ›real‹ Porsche, i.e. the six-cylinder. To rescue the situation, a four-cylinder project was born in the shape of the 912, which came out quickly on the heels of the 911.«

The decision to bring out a four-cylinder alongside the six-cylinder variant turned out to be the right one, because many buyers liked the shape of the 911, but did not really want that much power. The result was no less than 6401 buyers opting for a 912 the year it was introduced; exceeding the sales figures for the 911 by more than 100 percent. Over time, however, the 911 won the upper hand – nevertheless, of the 912, a total of 27 738 Coupes and 2562 Targas were built and sold.

But Porsche had another problem to solve – coachbuilder Reutter, which was building the chassis and bodyshell, was having more problems financing the investment costs due for the production of the 901. These were costs that Reutter did not really want to take on, because Reutter senior and junior had both died in the war and the eight remaining Reutter heirs saw themselves less as entrepreneurs and had, instead, appointed a CEO from outside the family. He had expertly driven the cooperation with Porsche and maximized volumes, turnover and profits. However, when it came to the production equipment for the 901, the enthusiasm evaporated. Karl Ludvigsen wrote, »When faced with the need to increase their investment in the company, the Reutter

heirs balked. Wary of even deeper involvement they decided, on the advice of their manager, to look for a buyer for the coachbuilding branch of the company in Zuffenhausen. They kept the original building on the Augustenstrasse in Stuttgart, forming there the Recaro GmbH and Company to continue making seats and seat adjusters.«

Porsche was the obvious candidate for acquiring Reutter in Zuffenhausen. The decision to buy was a difficult one, and Ferry Porsche spent a long time deliberating it. »We spent millions, and everything stayed the same as it was. We had to make an investment in something that brought us nothing new,« he said, and lashed out that they had previously been able to buy the necessary bodyshells from Reutter and had always been satisfied with them. In addition, German tax law made it difficult for Porsche to raise the capital necessary for an acquisition of this size. »Two thirds of our profits always went to the state,« said Ferry Porsche.

In the end, however, Porsche bought Reutter in July 1963. It changed little in Zuffenhausen. The Reutter factory remained as a stand-alone unit and continued to be managed by employees who saw themselves more as Reutter than as Porsche people. Porsche was nevertheless able to make a slight saving. Previously, sales of bodyshells from Reutter to Porsche had been subject to taxation of four percent; this disappeared after the sale. It was a miniscule relief compared with the extremely expensive acquisition of the Reutter coachworks and its 1000 employees. Porsche itself barely employed more at the end of 1963 – 1372 to be exact.

In addition to the costs of the Reutter takeover, Porsche also spent a further six million Deutschmarks in 1963 on new buildings and production equipment – more than twice as much than in the previous year. This expenditure was in preparation for the production of the 901, the start-up costs for which stood at around 15 million Marks. These impending costs were one of the main reasons why the Formula 1 program was not continued in 1963, despite its reasonable results in 1962. Porsche was being squeezed from several sides – it was a good thing that the team was so motivated and that the many development contracts were so lucrative.

But it was not just about the bodyshell, engine and gearbox – F. A. Porsche was also working in 1963 on bodyshell variants like a coupe with a sliding roof, a coupe with a rigid rollover bar and a removable steel roof (which would later become the Targa), a coupe with a folding roof and two cabriolet variants. Ferry Porsche had made it perfectly clear from the start that he wanted to see a cabriolet alongside the coupe in the lineup. However, time pressure – and probably also the lack of additional funds – made sure that it stayed with the coupe and the Targa, which was introduced two years later. In parallel, the dashboard was reconfigured from having two dials to the version with five dials that remains valid to this day – naturally, with the rev counter displayed prominently in the center. The instrument panel was also set five degrees steeper to address light reflection issues.

When Paul Hensler says today of the 901 or 911 that »every single part of this new design has its own story to tell – every single detail was a struggle«, you also begin to understand why it took until August 25, 1964 for Hans Tomala to declare in a meeting that design work on the new car was virtually complete. And this was almost one year after Porsche had unveiled the car at the Frankfurt Motor Show. But interested buyers had to wait a little longer, because it was not until the Paris Motor Show in October 1964 that Porsche announced that the first customer cars would now be delivered toward the end of the year – more than one year late.

However, the highly active press department, lead by Fritz Huschke von Hanstein, had already lined up the first drive reports on the 901 in summer 1964 when he handed pre-production vehicles to selected journalists – such as Reinhard Seiffert from *auto motor und sport* (issue 8/64) or the gentlemen from Swiss *Automobil Revue* on April 16, 1964, who summed up, »The taster was enjoyable. We are now waiting for series production to get going.«

It was a good thing that, in the meantime, only insiders had recognized that there would be problems with the front axle. Hans Tomala had accepted the solution with the damper struts and torsion bar preferred by all involved, but selected a very simple – and cost-saving – approach that involved simply welding the top of the damper struts to the chassis. Not only did this quickly result in fatigue cracks, but also meant that there was no further scope here for fine tuning. Because of this fixing arrangement, it was no longer possible to set camber or caster offset, which led to merely average handling characteristics and made the car far more susceptible to cross winds. It may have saved on costs, but this measure leading to such distinctly un-Porsche-like handling was a thorn in the flesh of Ferdinand Piëch from the very start. He wrote in his *Auto.Biographie*, »The Tomala solution of a suspension strut that could not be adjusted from above was another botch job. It needed improvisation at the end of the welding work, and then on top of that the joint only held for five thousand kilometers.« Going on to add, »The problems the first 911 had with directional stability were dramatic enough, and I hated the dog's-dinner solution with that mess of iron in the corners of the bumpers. Within a reasonable timeframe, we had found engineering solutions of weight distribution and balance.«

How hard it was to weld these fixed damper struts in the correct place is evident today in the restoration of early 901s and 911s. Alois Ruf, the specialist Porsche tuner and restorer and independent vehicle maker, recalls

»THE TASTER WAS ENJOYABLE – WE ARE NOW WAITING FOR SERIES PRODUCTION TO GET GOING.«

many restoration vehicles from this era where »we are repeatedly amazed how often and how very many welding points and subsequent welding work we find – as if every car had had to be fine tuned again and again.«

What particularly irritated Ferdinand Piëch was the fact that »Tomala had signed off this rigid connection of the suspension strut with the bodyshell for series production without the approval of the Testing

HERE, THE VERY PLEASANT MR. FUCHS FROM THE VEHICLE FLEET IN LUDWIGSBURG DEMONSTRATES
HOW BIG THE TRUNK OF THE 901 ACTUALLY IS.

department, which obviously led to confrontation with me. I gave my uncle an ultimatum. Tomala went – I stayed. He was certainly not a bad technician, but too stubborn to allow his ideas to be tested against the current state-of-the-art.«

So the company adopted the interim solution, much hated by Piëch, of building added weight into the bumpers of the 911 – a solution which, by the way, was used only in the 911 with the six-cylinder engine; the lighter, four-cylinder engine in the 912 made this unnecessary. However, work progressed apace on reinforcing and adapting the upper fixing point in such a way as to permit the adjustment of camber and caster offset. The solution came into effect early in 1966 and made the much-derided additional weight superfluous.

Series production itself began September 14, 1964 with chassis number 300007, with chassis number 300001 not being built until three days later – and because this date was ahead of the Paris Motor Show, these vehicles were still built and designated as 901s. It would take until November 10, 1964 for the decision to change the 901 to the 911 to become official – all coupes built from this day on were true 911s. However, it is not surprising to hear that this decision, too, was not applied entirely consistently; as Tobias Aichele knows all too well, having researched the story of these chassis numbers in minute detail. »The changeover to 911 numbering took place on November 10, 1964 with vehicle chassis number 300049, i.e. prior to delivery of the first vehicles. But this did not mean that 49 vehicles were processed internally as 901, because – as is already evident from the first vehicles – the vehicles were not produced with chronologically sequential chassis numbers. Thus, vehicles 74 and 79 were already built with the internal designation 901 on November 5, 1964. A total of 82 vehicles were produced with the internal designation 901. We are now able to reconstruct the order and volumes of 911 production; allowing us to say definitively for the first time that exactly 232 vehicles were produced in 1964.«

This was the beginning of an unbelievable success story. When the 901 was first unveiled in Frankfurt in September 1963, the air-cooled, six-cylinder engine had a displacement of 1991 cm^3 and produced exactly 130 hp or 96 kW at 6100 rpm. Its maximum torque stood at 175 Nm, which it delivered at 4200 rpm. Contact with the road was supplied by 165 VR 15 tires mounted on 4.5 x 15-inch rims. The fact that this power unit had no problem producing increasing amounts of power over the decades that followed is in no small part due to the extensive involvement in its design and ongoing development during these years of Ferdinand Piëch. Until the completion of his studies at ETH Zürich, Ferdinand Piëch worked during his holidays in Stuttgart and, from April 1964, was at the company full time. Due not least to his family connections, he succeeded in implementing everything that made the six-cylinder something special from the very start of its career – from the dry-sump lubrication to the very best materials.

Nobody could possibly have imagined that the successor to the 356 would be celebrated as an icon – for half a century now – as an aesthetic milestone, as one of the world's great sports cars and as the victor of countless rallies and races. The Carrera GT 2 RS now delivers no less than 620 hp – an unimaginable figure back then, and still impressive today. The 901 may have had a difficult birth, but it captured the imagination from the very start and overcame its weaknesses with remarkable aplomb. And it became synonymous with sporty driving and everyday usability – a mixture that can't necessarily be taken for granted with sports cars.

HOW THE 901 *BECAME* THE 911

NOBODY *REALLY* KNOWS

Plenty has been written about how the 901 became the 911 – Peugeot saw the Porsche 901 at the Paris Motor Show, which took place from October 3 to 13, 1964, and wrote a letter to Ferry Porsche. In it, they respectfully requested the removal of the zero in the model designation, as this had been a tradition of the cars from Sochaux

---

are overwritten in pencil with a one, turning the 901 into 911 and the 902 into 912. What is interesting about this is the date – it is the opening date of the Paris Motor Show. As a side note, the plan was for the Reutter coachworks to build 2000 units of the 901 (six-cylinder), 2200 units of the 902 (4-cylinder) and 1000 open cars, behind which lurked the full cabriolet, which was still on the Sales department wish list at this point. A further 4000 units of the 902 were planned to be built by Karmann.

And let's also clarify why Porsche began to use the new number nine from this project onward. Karl Ludvigsen writes on this topic, »It has been an article of faith among Porsche enthusiasts that the 901 type number was applied because the car design was the 901st project in the sequence of studies undertaken by the Porsche design office since its founding in 1930. But such was not the case.

Over the years Porsche skipped many numbers in the sequence. Sometimes the omissions were accidental, for Karl Rabe, the keeper of the numbers, was anything but methodical in their allocation. Sometimes the omissions were deliberate, as when the men of Porsche decided to begin with No. 7, so that their first customer, the Wanderer Werke, would not think that they were a bunch of novices. During the hectic war years many numbers in the 200 series were skipped. In the 400 series only six numbers were used, the last being 425; a fresh start was made at 500 when the design office moved back to Stuttgart.

From 500 onward the type-number list was relatively tightly packed through the 700s and into the early 800s, the Type 804 Grand Prix car being an example. That was where the list stood when the time came to pick a number for the successor to the 356. To get it they jumped over many 800-series numbers and picked 901. Why? To symbolize a new beginning with a new model? To get an attractively well-rounded number? The real reason was much more prosaic.

In the early 1960s Porsche was more closely integrating its sales, parts and service operations with those of Volkswagen. In fact a joint VW-Porsche sports-car sales program was not too many years in the future. Porsche part numbers, therefore, needed to become compatible with those used by VW, and when a review was made of the number classes that were already in use on the Wolfsburg parts-control computers it turned out that the only category that was still free was the 900 series. That was why the new Porsche was named the 901, at first, and why all subsequent Porsches have been numbered in the 900s.«

since 1929. On the basis of this, Porsche renamed the 901 the 911 – while the 902 mutated into the 912. So far, so good – but there are a few catches in the story.

Let's first establish why Porsche opted for the digit sequence 901 for this new model range – but, in order to do that, we must clarify the date on which the model designation was changed from 901 to 911. The numeric sequence 911/912 appears for the first time in a letter dated October 3, 1964, which outlines the »proposals for the follow-up contract for 901/902 bodyshells«. On this internal memo, the two zeros in 901 and 902

THE FATHERS OF THE 901 FROM LEFT TO RIGHT — OR MOST OF THEM AT LEAST: FRANZ XAVER REIMSPIESS,
KARL RUOFF, RICHARD HETMANN, LEOPOLD JÄNTSCHKE, ERICH STOTZ, HANS HERZOG, ROBERT BINDER,
HANS HÖNICK, RUDOLF HOFMANN, ALFRED KÜHN, WALTER BEIERBACH, THEO BAUER, ERWIN KOMENDA,
WILHELM ALBRECHT, GOTTLOB STURM, HANS TOMALA, GERHARD SCHRÖDER, KARL MOZELT, HANS MEZGER,
KARL MEZGER, ERNST WEYERSBERG, HERBERT LINGE, DR. FERRY PORSCHE, KURT KNOERZER (BACK),
KARL SCHILLING, FERDINAND PIËCH, ADOLF SCHNEIDER, F. A. PORSCHE, HELMUT ROMBOLD.

With the introduction of the Type 901, the Porsche Company has added another car to round off the upper end of their current program of fast and economical automobiles. The new model was designed in the best of Porsche tradition, combining the virtues of the well proven Type 356 models with ideas and experience gathered by the technical staff of designers and development engineers over a period of many years. Being equal to the Carrera 2000 GS in weight and temperament, and even excelling it in top speed, the Type 901 will again demonstrate that in a Porsche driving is at its best. This car will provide unequalled driving comfort, handling, and safety — qualities which the demanding Porsche owner has enjoyed ever since the introduction of the first Porsche.

The engine is an air cooled, opposed six cylinder unit with one camshaft for each bank of cylinders (ohc). Applied in this design are concepts conceived and proven in the course of development of Grand Prix engines and high performance sports car engines. The crankshaft is mounted in eight main bearings. Component parts are, to

901

PLAIN, SIMPLE AND PACKED WITH
TECHNICAL DETAILS — THE FIRST 901
BROCHURE.

Technical Data

Engine

Number of cylinders	6
Bore	80 mm (3.15 in.)
Stroke	66 mm (2.60 in.)
Piston displacement, actual	1991 cc (121.5 cu. in.)
Compression ratio	9:1
Horsepower rating	130 HP (DIN) at 6200 rpm
Maximum torque	16.5 mkg at 4600 rpm
	119.3 lbs/ft at 4600 rpm
Horsepower per liter	65 HP (DIN)

Engine Design Data

Engine type	Horizontally opposed six, carburetor type, four stroke cycle
Cooling system	Air cooled
Crankcase	Light alloy
Cylinders	Cast iron
Cylinder heads	Light alloy
Number of valves per cylinder	1 intake, 1 exhaust
Valve arrangement	overhead in "V", hemispherical combustion chamber
Camshafts	OHC, in cylinder heads
Valve timing	Over rocker arms
Camshaft drive	By chain
Crankshaft	Forged steel, 8 main bearings
Connecting rod bearings	Plain journal bearings
Blower drive	By V-belt
Lubrication system	Dry sump (separate oil tank); full pressure; with scavenger pump; full-flow oil cooler and oil filter
Fuel supply	Electric fuel pump
Electrical system	12 volt, 45 Ah battery
Radio interference suppression	Accomplished in accordance with VDE 0879, Part I

a large degree, of light alloy. This engine was designed with due consideration towards its adaptability for competition use in appropriate stages of development. The two camshafts are chain-driven, a feature applied in Porsches for the first time. A new transmission has been designed for this car. Although similar to the previous units in mechanical operation, the new transmission has five forward speeds to cope with the extended speed range.

The front wheel suspension consists of the shockabsorbers and low positioned transverse control arms, with springing effected by longitudinal torsion bars. Suspension of the rear wheels is by longitudinal control arms with transverse torsion bars. Power is transmitted to the rear wheels by twin-joint half-axles.

The rack-and-pinion steering is positioned in the forward center of the vehicle. Owing to this arrangement, which necessiated the utilization of relay shafts in place of a solid steering rod, the aspect of interior safety has been greatly enhanced. The car is equipped with disc brakes on all four wheels.

In view of considerations given to body dimensions, it became necessary to consolidate the new components into a compact unit. The inside space has been enlarged while keeping the outside dimensions down – here exceeding the overall length of the Type 356 by only 120 mm, yet reducing the overall width by 70 mm. At the same time larger window areas have been provided, to satisfy the demands of today.

Despite of the reduced overall width, it was possible to widen the forward passenger space. Retained basically unchanged is the seating arrangement which provides utmost comfort on long distance trips. Leg room behind the forward seats has been extended by approximately 6 cm. Both front fenders have been made detachable to simplify repairs.

A special effort was made to provide an adequate solution to interior ventilation. The spacious luggage compartment under the front hood of the car provides adequate space for the accomodation of suitcases and other luggage.

Generator	360 watt, with current and voltage regulator	Hand brake drum diameter	180 mm (7.1 in.)
Ignition type	Battery coil	Total sweep area	194 cm² (30.1 sq. in.)
		Tires	165 x 15, braced tread
Power Train		Rim type	4¹/₂ J x 15
Location of engine in vehicle	At rear, behind rear axle	Steering	Rack-and-pinion; steering damper;
Clutch	Single plate, dry, diaphragm type		safety steering post (by relay)
Transmission	Porsche, servo-thrust synchronization	Steering ratio	1:17
Number of speeds	5 forward, 1 reverse	Fuel tank capacity	approx. 68 liters (18.0 US gallons or
Synchronized gears	1 through 5		15.0 Imperial gallons)
Location of gearshift lever	On floor in center of vehicle		
	(besides driver's seat)	**Performance**	
Final drive	Spiral bevel gears in final drive;	Maximum speed	approx. 210 kmh (130 mph)
	conventional differential; limited-slip	Weight/power ratio (ready to operate)	7.7 kg/HP (DIN)
	bevel gear differential; limited-slip	Fuel consumption	11–14 liters per 100 km (17–21 miles/US gal,
Axle ratio	7 : 31, i = 4.428		or 20–26 miles/Imperial gallon)
Gear ratios	See table below	Acceleration 0–100 kmh (0–62.1 mph)	9.1 sec.
		0–160 kmh (0–99.4 mph)	21.9 sec.
Chassis and Suspension		Elapsed time for 1 km	29.9 sec. (standing start)
Frame (Underbody)	Welded, pressed-steel sections	for 400 m (¹/₄ mile)	16.4 sec.
	unitized with body		
Front wheel suspension	Independent wheel suspension with	**Dimensions**	
	transverse control arms, and guide struts	Wheelbase	2204 mm (86.77 in.)
Front wheel springing	By torsion bars and rubber cushions	Track, front	1332 mm (52.44 in.)
Rear wheel suspension	Independent wheel suspension with	Track, rear	1312 mm (51.65 in.)
	longitudinal control arms	Overall length	4135 mm (162.8 in.)
Rear wheel springing	By torsion bars and rubber cushions	Overall width	1600 mm (62.99 in.)
Shockabsorbers	Hydraulic, double-action telescopic	Overall height	1273 mm (50.12 in.)
	shockabsorbers front and rear	Ground clearance	118 mm (4.65 in.)
Service brakes	Four wheel, hydraulic disc brakes	Turning circle	10 m (32.8 ft.)
Hand brake	Mechanical, acting on rear wheels		
Effective brake disc dia. front	227 mm (8.94 in.)	**Gear Ratios**	
rear	243 mm (9.57 in.)	5-speed transmission	1st gear (11 : 34) i = 3.09
Brake lining area, per wheel			2nd gear (18 : 34) i = 1.89
front	52.5 cm² (8.14 sq. in.)		3rd gear (22 : 29) i = 1.32
rear	40 cm² (6.20 sq. in.)		4th gear (26 : 26) i = 1.0
Total brake sweep area	185 cm² (28.68 sq. in.)		5th gear (29 : 22) i = 0.758
			Additional gear sets are available.

NOBODY HAD ACTUALLY SEEN A LETTER FROM PEUGEOT CONCERNING THE 901.

London Motor Show and all the big automotive publications presented their first-drive reports on the 901. And yet Porsche changed the name from 901/902 to 911/912 in a matter of days.

Today, it is no longer possible to establish what actually happened, as neither the Porsche nor the Peugeot archive now holds the original or the copy of that ominous court order asserting the right to all model designations with a zero in the middle of a three-figure number. And, although all eye-witnesses spoken to tell of this letter, none of them has actually seen and read it. Everyone knows about it only from hearsay and from statements made by others who claim to have seen this document. Yet you might reasonably assume that a letter of such significance – passed from board member to board member – would have been kept in the company files.

Probably – and this is purely speculation – the Peugeot demand was never made at the highest level or with the threat of some kind of consequences. Probably, Peugeot approached Porsche about this, and Porsche had absolutely no intention of getting itself into trouble in France – at the time its third-biggest market – with one of the market leaders. They simply opted to avoid any possible difficulties and changed the model name to 911.

As far as the 904 Carrera GTS was concerned, however, Peugeot's chances were not good; the car had already been on the market for almost a year. Nevertheless, it was argued that this mid-engine race car was not a series-production model and would therefore not be a competitor to anything in the French company's extensive model range. It was an assertion that immediately moved Head of Porsche Racing Fritz Huschke von Hanstein to name subsequent race cars from Zuffenhausen with model designations like 906, 907, 908 and 909 – against which Peugeot made no protest whatsoever.

Thus, the first project in this new (possible) cooperation was allocated with the first number in this 900 series – 901. Further models appeared in parallel, such as the 904 Carrera GTS, which was developed alongside the 901 as a mid-engine sports car and celebrated its premiere on November 26, 1963 on the Solitude Race Track.

It is interesting to note that Peugeot had nothing against the use of the designation 904 Carrera GTS, although there is also a zero in its model name – it was a further eleven months before the 901 made its French debut at the Paris Motor Show and Peugeot woke up and formulated its request. These were eleven months during which the 901 also appeared at the

The fact remains, however, that several 901 vehicles had already been built by this time and used as test vehicles. A few models even made it into the hands of selected dealerships as demonstrator vehicles – and particularly trusted employees were also able to acquire the occasional 901. But they had to undertake not to sell on the vehicles as it could lead, with some justification, to problems with Peugeot if a 901 were officially to be offered for sale. Thus, the tracks of the 911 predecessor were lost over the years – and, to this day, only a very few of these rarities have resurfaced.

HOW CAN YOU TELL THE DIFFERENCE BETWEEN A 901 AND A 911? THE 911 HAS A CHROME STRIP BENEATH THE DOOR THAT IS NOT FEATURED IN THE 901 BROCHURE – ALTHOUGH IT WAS INCLUDED ON MANY 901S.

PORSCHE **901**

PORSCHE

Qualität durch Erfahrung — das war bei der Entwicklung des Typs 911 der Grundsatz der Porsche-Konstrukteure.

Ein exklusiver in allen Geschwindigkeitsbereichen ideal abgestufter Reisewagen verwandelt sich, zügig gefahren, in ein sportliches Coupé europäischer Elite.

Nicht Transport oder Repräsentation, sondern das beglückende Gefühl — Fahren um des Fahrens willen — begründet die alte Porsche-Formel „Fahren in seiner schönsten Form".

Excellence through experience — the maxim guiding Porsche designers in their work on Type 911.

An exclusive touring car, with its perfectly graduated speed ranges, it converts into a sporting coupe of the European elite.

The traditional Porsche slogan "Driving at its finest" expresses not simply the quality of movement or mechanism, but the joy of driving for its own sake.

La qualité grâce à l'expérience — tel fut le principe fondamental des usines Porsche lors de l'étude du type 911.

Une voiture de tourisme exceptionnelle, idéale et bien adaptée à tous les régimes, se transformant, lorsqu'elle est conduite rapidement, en un coupé sportif de standing européen.

Ce n'est pas son côté utilitaire ni son bel aspect, mais la sensation merveilleuse éprouvée à «conduire pour la joie de conduire» qui a créé le vieux slogan de Porsche: «Joie de conduire dans sa plus belle expression».

PORSCHE **911**

THE PROTOTYPE LIST

Porsche never actually delivered a series-production 911 with the model name 901. The veto from Peugeot against the 901 model name came directly after the Paris Motor Show in October 1964 and the first 911s were delivered to the foreign and domestic dealer organization in Zuffenhausen on November 16 and 17 of that year. The first private customers took delivery a few days later.

1962 – 1964:
901/911-
PROTOTYPES

FERRY PORSCHE WITH HIS SECRETARY HELENE WERKMEISTER
AND HIS 901 IN WORKS I IN 1964 (CHASSIS NO. 300003).

All the vehicles already had the model name 911 and a »3« at the beginning of every chassis number. Thus, a car with the chassis number 300012, for instance, is the twelfth series-production 911 ever produced.

More precise differentiation is, however, required within the company. The first series-production body-shell with the chassis number 300007 left the production line on September 14, 1964. Interestingly, the first chassis number was not produced until September 17, 1964. Because the production of these first vehicles took place before the Peugeot veto, the vehicles were still referred to internally as 901. The change to the 911 numbering happened on November 10, 1964 with chassis number 300049, still before delivery of the first vehicles. But this does not mean that 49 vehicles were handled internally as 901, because – as already indicated by the first vehicles – the cars were not produced with chronologically sequential chassis numbers. Thus, vehicles 74 and 79 with the internal reference 901 were built on November 5, 1964. A total of 82 vehicles ran internally under the designation 901.

The order and volumes of 911 production can be reconstructed with the help of some intensive research. We can also now say for sure that exactly 232 vehicles were built in 1964. The last car of the year had chassis number 233 and was assembled on December 23, 1964. The first of the following year, with the number 235, received its identification on January 4.

In terms of equipment, however, there was absolutely no difference between the vehicles referred to internally as 901 and the vehicles produced as 911s as of November 10, 1964. Starting with the first chassis number, this was the so-called 0 series, which was produced until the end of July 1965. This designation is incredibly misleading, as automotive construction usually differentiates stages as follows: The first vehicles are prototypes that are built almost entirely by hand.

These are followed by pre-production cars, built for the purposes of functional testing. Then comes the 0 series – also known as nil series – which uses, if possible, only series-production components. These vehicles, of which there are usually around 50, are built entirely using the production equipment of the subsequent series cars.

In the case of the Porsche 911, however, the 0 series refers not only to these vehicles, but to the entire first vehicle generation prior to the so-called A series (like 356 – 356 A). Nowadays, letter identifiers have been standardized throughout the automotive industry in order to simplify classification.

The vehicles built within the first series of 911 require further subdivision. Following the first year of production, which ended with the plant's summer shut-down in August 1965, the vehicles had a large number of new details. The last chassis number that could be defined as an Ur-911 car of the first model year was 302104. This car was produced with 13 others on July 30, 1965. The first chassis number to be built on August 16, 1965 following the plant shut-down was 302114.

To sum up, we can say that all vehicles produced between September 14, 1964 and July 30, 1965 were production-identical Ur-911s. The true 901s are prototypes with the chassis numbers of the so-called replacement bodyshells that begin with a »13«. The first 901 test car had the chassis number 13321. However, these early versions were chronologically numbered only until the tenth vehicle. The eleventh vehicle departed from the sequence again with the chassis number 13352. With chassis number 300001, the twelfth test car already carried the first series-production number.

Earlier records show how many prototypes there were and to what they were subjected. In order to clarify eye-witness accounts of the 911 development, the data on every single vehicle was gathered together for the first time for the work *Porsche 911 – Forever young*. In compiling it, the author used as his reference the records produced by the Testing department. There were, of course, significantly more than the 13 prototypes listed, but these cars told the story of the 911 through to delivery of the first series-production vehicles. These also include vehicles 12 and 13, although they already bore series-production numbers.

RALLYE MONTE CARLO – PORSCHE RACING DRIVER HERBERT LINGE AND PROTOTYPE NO. 13 (CHASSIS NO. 300002) IN JANUARY 1965.

The author took the liberty of withholding an identifying feature of each car in order to be able to expose a replica of a prototype at any given time. Furthermore, for data protection reasons, only Porsche employees were identified as buyers, although private customers are also known to exist. This makes it possible to reconstruct the whereabouts of every single 901 until it was scrapped. This information was, however, only seldom itemized. Car number seven survived and was restored in the USA. Its interesting and unusual story, entitled »Number 7 is alive«, is told in detail on pages 149 to 155.

This information came from a number of different sources. Heinrich Klie, who was the individual in the Bodyshell department responsible for liaison between Engineering, Production and Testing, kept records on the sequencing of chassis numbers for the prototypes.

Head of Test Driving Helmuth Bott maintained records for the Testing function. A list dated July 29, 1963 mentions the first seven vehicles. In addition, Helmuth Bott also started a list of test cars in January 1964 that he continuously updated on a monthly rota through the end of 1965. From this, we can derive the kilometers on the clock and the use of every single vehicle. Helmuth Bott also kept separate records in 1965 on the respective tested fuel consumption. Further information can be drawn from the mentioned T8 meetings, Thursday meetings and technical meetings referenced.

Because a report dated March 2, 1964 detailing the development status of the engines was preserved, individual engine numbers could even be attributed to the prototypes. Thus, factual information on each prototype came together and was cross-referenced by Helmuth Bott with his personal files from the period.

Unearthing visual images of the individual vehicles proved especially difficult as there was obviously a strict photography ban at the time in every one of the departments. Here, too, it has only been possible to compile an interesting smorgasbord with a great deal of legwork and using private photos shot secretly by employees at the time. On top of that, Helmuth Bott had a previously unpublished film stored under lock and key that he shot in the early 1960s during test drives.

In a laborious process, this film material was used to generate and classify photos of the prototypes. This classification was exacerbated by the fact that the prototypes had only temporary number plates for parts of their lives. Vehicles number two and three were even disguised with American number plates. What the 911 prototypes had in common was the structure of their chassis numbers. They began with 1332 and were differentiated only by their end number. Thus, the chassis number of the very first car was, as previously mentioned, 13321.

There were seven prototypes leading up to the start of series production (13321 through 13327). Then came two 912 test cars (initially called 902) with the numbers 13328 and 13329. A further four prototypes (13330 through 13333) were built before the end of 1964.

Basically, the prototypes differed visually from the later series-production cars in the absence of bumper guards, the lack of sill trim and the missing lettering on the rear lid. Some of the cars, however, were fitted retrospectively with a few of these components in the years that followed. The respective details are listed as follows.

NUMBER 1 (901/1) (911)*

Chassis number: 13321

Color: white

Registration: never assigned

Nickname: »Sturmvogel« (»Petrel«)

Body manufactured by: Reutter;
Platform Porsche

Year: 1962

Intended use: presentations and inspections; wind tunnel; later mainly braking and carburetor tests

Front axle: subframe

Rear axle: 356 B (swing axle)

Brakes: Girling

Engine: S 90; later 901

Engine number: 08

Transmission number: 741/2A, No. 304 (4-speed); ratios**: 11/34, 17/30, 23/26, 27/22

Assembly: body by September 14, 1962; suspension and driveline in Testing department shed; mechanics: Albert Junginger, Walter Bemsel (electrics)

Uses: in July 1963 car only slowly rollable; 02/27/64 on-road testing with alloy wheel; early 1964, brake testing; February 1965, testing rear swing axle at 25 200 km; carburetor tests

Fate: destroyed in early 1965 at the end of carburetor tests

* *from November 1964*
** *from 1st to 4th or 5th gear resp.*

NUMBER 2 (901/2) (911/2)

Chassis number: 13322

Color: white; camouflaged with German army-style olive-grey wax;

Registration: HEC 626 (USA, yellow); temporary German registration S-04324

Nickname: »Fledermaus« (»Bat«)

Body manufactured by: Reutter

Year: 1963

Intended use: body and engine testing; heating, suspension and carburetor tests

Front axle: subframe

Rear axle: 901 (trailing arm) preliminary

Brakes: Girling, later Teves

Engine: 901 without dry-sump lubrication, 821 timing gear, crossflow carburetor

Engine number: 900003 (destroyed), later 900012

Transmission number: 741/2A, No. 52637 (4-speed); ratios: 11/34, 17/30, 23/26, 27/23

Equipment: old exterior mirrors by Mall (644-731.111.06); Webasto engine heater; single bucket seat mounted sideways in rear on 11/19/63, first version of engine hood louvers

Assembly: body by October 12, 1962; suspension and driveline in Testing department shed; mechanics: Albert Junginger, Walter Bemsel (electrics)

Miscellaneous: dry weight 1065 kg; fuel consumption 14.5 liters per 100 km

Uses: first »staged« press picture taken between Weilimdorf and Münchingen; heating tests with Webasto on 02/27/64; test drives between 06/10/63 and 07/11/63 (negative pressure measurements inside and in engine compartment); tests at Nürburgring from 07/01/63 to 07/05/63; heater tests in early 1964 at km 5900; wind tunnel test on 14/02/64; brake tests on 06/10/64

Fate: destroyed in late 1964

WHILE THE WHITE 901 IS ONE OF THE PRE-SERIES CARS, THE RED CAR IS PROTOTYPE NUMBER 3, NICKNAMED »BLAUMEISE« (»BLUE TIT«, NO. 13323),
LATER REPAINTED. THE TWO BOTTOM IMAGES SHOW S-SK 726 – THE »ZITRONENFALTER« (»BRIMSTONE BUTTERFLY«).

NUMBER 3 (901/3) (911/3)

Chassis number: 13323

Color: dark blue; partially camouflaged with German army-style olive-grey wax; repainted red on 05/27/64

Registration: HEC 627 (USA, yellow); as of February 1964 S-SK 725; from 1965 on no registration

Nickname: »Blaumeise« (»Blue Tit«)

Body manufactured by: Porsche by Heinz Fuchs; Platform Porsche

Year: 1963

Intended use: suspension development; test car for endurance and wind tunnel testing in Wolfsburg

Front axle: 901 (subframe)

Rear axle: 901

Brakes: Girling, later Teves

Engine: 901 with dry-sump lubrication, brought up-to-date in January 1964; engine damaged on 03/05/64; crossflow carburetor with intake filter by Knecht, comparisons with triple Solex float carburetor

Engine number: 05; later 04 with 145 hp at 6300 rpm

Transmission number: 901, No. 2 (5-speed); ratios: 14/37, 19/32, 23/28, 26/25, 28/23

Equipment: sample mirror by Mall attached to door window frame; no heater

Assembly: by July 31, 1963

Uses: 09/24/63 to 10/05/63 VW test track in Wolfsburg; 11/08/63 performance tests; endurance testing at 15 259 km in early 1964; as of 04/15/64 completely disassembled and stripped (at 45 000 km incl. 6500 km on Weissach test track); end of 1964 engine type 1/64 and Boge »Hydromat« dampers installed; carburetor tests from 03/01/65; on 05/27/64 in body shop for updating and repainting (red); June 1965 engine tests at 29 775 km (new speedometer); as of September 1965 on VW's books

Fate: unknown

NUMBER 4 (901/4) (911/4)

Chassis number: 13324

Color: yellow

Registration: temporary registration S-04326; S-SK 726 (from February 1964); since June 1965 without registration number; from September 1965 registered and insured by Teves

Nickname: »Zitronenfalter« (»Brimstone Butterfly«)

Body manufactured by: Porsche; Platform Porsche

Year: 1963

Intended use: motor show back-up; originally intended as display car for Frankfurt Motor Show

Front axle: 901 (new development status as of July 25, 1963)

Rear axle: 901

Brakes: Girling, later Teves

Engine: 901 with dry sump lubrication (115.9 hp at 5500 rpm)

Engine number: 07; damaged 06/08/64; from 11/02/65 2195 cm³ engine delivering 170 hp (at 6500 rpm)

Transmission number: 901, No. 4 (5-speed); ratios: 11/34, 18/33, 23/28, 26/25, 28/23

Equipment: sample mirror from Fechenbacher; with Webasto and without engine heating; battery in front

Assembly: August 1963

Miscellaneous: dry weight 1086 kg; tank capacity 62 liters; fuel consumption 21.8 liters

Uses: first exhibitions, then test car; early 1963 suspension tests at km 6916; 03/19/64 modified front axle with short springs and new subframe; late 1964 brake tests by Teves; June 1965 transmission test at 62 000 km; August 1965 brake tests at Teves (car on loan)

Fate: unknown

NUMBER 5 (901/5) (911/5)

Chassis number: 13325

Color: yellow

Registration: early 1964 without, then S-TC 1; no longer registered after September 1965

Nickname: none

Body manufactured by: Karmann; Platform Porsche

Year: 1963

Intended use: first of the display cars; demonstrator; test car (carburetors); sales

Front axle: 901

Rear axle: 901

Brakes: Girling

Engine: first engine dummy, then 901 with dry-sump lubrication

Engine number: 11 (overhauled at km 31 900), then No. 15

Transmission number: 901, No. 3 (5-speed); ratios: 11/34 (later 14/37), 18/33 (later 19/32), 23/28, 26/25, 28/23; crown-wheel and pinion 7/31

Equipment: circular instruments and steering wheel from 356; Webasto heater; from 1965 on with air condition

Assembly: August 1963

Miscellaneous: dry weight 1059 kg; oil consumption ca. 1.5 l per 1000 km; fuel consumption 14.3 l per 100 km

Uses: from September 12, 1963 Frankfurt Motor Show; October 3 to 13, 1963 Paris Motor Show; October 16 to 26, 1963 London Motor Show; October 30 to November 10, 1963 Turin Motor Show; Early February 1964 noise measurements, then sales tour with Dieter Lenz over 50 000 km; at Geneva Motor Show at 17 250 km; first prototype to be tested by *auto motor und sport* (issue 8/1964); mid-September 1964 support vehicle for Tour de France (drivers von Hanstein and Barth); tire testing on Hockenheimring (09/29/64 to 10/01/64); then carburetor tests; tests with automatic transmission late 1964 to August 1965 up to 76 100 km

Fate: destroyed after an accident during transmission testing on 12/07/65

NUMBER 6 (901/6) (911/6)

Chassis number: 13326

Color: Emailblau 6403 (Enamel Blue)

Nickname: »Quickblau«

Body manufactured by: Karmann;
Platform Porsche

Intended use: sales, exhibitions, foreign markets

Front axle: 901

Rear axle: 901

Brakes: Girling or Teves (depending on parts available, as in memo dated July 25, 1963)

Engine: first engine dummy; from May 1964, 901 with dry-sump lubrication

Engine number: 09; later 154

Transmission number: 901, No. 1 (5-speed); ratios: 11/34, 18/33, 22/29, 26/26, 29/22

Equipment: new dashboard with five dials; Rosanil 705 leather; black seats with hounds-tooth center stripes (7/127); leather door panels; carpets made in Besmer velours IDEE 903

Assembly: September 1963

Uses: Motor Shows in London (October 16 to 26, 1963) and Sweden, Berlin and Geneva; from mid-1963 first car to be converted to demonstrator, finished January 1964; was supposed to be road-ready in March 1964; tire tests on Hockenheimring (09/29/64. to 10/01/64); bought privately and driven by Ferdinand Piëch (in September 1965), handed to Hans Mezger on 12/30/65; on 12/12/67 showed a total of 63 381 km.

Fate: unknown

NUMBER 7 (901/7) (911/7)

Chassis number: 13327

Color: Signalrot (Signal Red)

Registration: S-SX 564 (from February 1964)

Nickname: »Barbarossa«

Body manufactured by: Porsche

Platform Porsche

Year: 1963

Intended use: testing: wind tunnel; homologation (finished July 9, 1964)

Front axle: 901

Rear axle: 901

Brakes: Teves

Engine: engine installed 04/10/64; 901 with dry-sump lubrication (126 hp at 6300 rpm); cast iron cylinders; engine number: 14

Transmission number: 901, No. 6 (5-speed); ratios: 11/34, 18/33, 23/28, 26/25, 28/23; transmission change on July 9, 1964

Equipment: two instrument dials, similar to type 356 (150 mm diameter instead of 100 mm); steering wheel and horn ring also similar to 356; old exterior mirrors from Mall (901.731.111.00)

Assembly: September 1963

Miscellaneous: turning circle: left 10.16 m, right 9.70 m; dry weight 1084 kg

Uses: February 1964 suspension testing at 1369 km; after that wind tunnel tests; on 03/19/64 modification to front axle with flanbloc bushings resulted in significantly improved stability; from 11/05/64 reverted to series parts; from December 1964 brake testing at 36 000 km; February 1965 suspension test (front axle) at 40 000 km; on 10/15/65 odometer read 43 927 km

Fate: in April 1965, No. 7 was bought by Richard von Frankenberg, who kept it until September 26, 1966; then lost for some time in Italy; resurfaced in the early 1960s in New York; sold to Pennsylvania; restored for the 1993 New York Auto Show.

PROTOTYPE NUMBER 6 – »QUICKBLAU« – WAS THE STAR OF THE GENEVA MOTOR SHOW 1964. BELOW, TWO PRE-SERIES 901S NEAR ESSLINGEN AND IN THE FACTORY YARD. BOTTOM: PROTOTYPE NUMBER 7, NICKNAMED »BARBAROSSA«.

NUMBER 8 (911/8)

Chassis number: 13328
Color: brown with front trunk lid offset in red
Registration: S-TV 112 (from July 1964)
Nickname: none
Body finished by December 1963;
delivery in June 1964
Year: 1964
Intended use: testing; homologation
Front axle: 901
Rear axle: 901
Brakes: Teves
Engine: 901 with dry-sump lubrication;
from August 1965 four-cylinder engine 616/36
Engine number: 901; from August 1965 VW
automatic transmission EA 080/3-IV
(Porsche type 903/2)
Equipment: longer window frames for testing;
with Webasto and engine heater; battery in
front; new dashboard with five instrument dials
and wooden steering wheel
Assembly: unknown
Miscellaneous: turning circle left 9.95 m, right
11.08 m; dry weight 1066 kg; fuel consumption
22.2 liters; top speed 214 km/h (measured on
13 July 1964)
Uses: body ready on 04/10/64; mid-1964
suspension testing; July 1964 endurance testing
at 3000 km; August 1964 training run to Tour
de France; from 08/20/64 Alpenfahrt with
Herbert Linge; tire tests at Hockenheimring
(09/21/64 to 10/01/64); tests with Weber
carburetors in December 1964 at 40 000 km;
brake tests from January 1965 at 43 000 km;
from 06/01/64 to 06/15/64 »tougher circuit«
in Wolfsburg; June 1965 transmission tests at
47 500 km
Fate: sold on 04/18/68

NUMBER 9 (911/9)

Chassis number: 13329
Color: unknown
Registration: S-UE 87
Nickname: none
Body manufactured by: Reutter
Year: 1964
Intended use: sales demonstrator; homologation
for Italy (November 1964); body tests
Front axle: 901
Rear axle: 901
Brakes: Teves
Engine: 901 with dry-sump lubrication;
later four-cylinder type 616/36
Engine number: unknown
Equipment: electric sunroof (plus 10 kg),
hinged front wind deflector over the entire
width; Webasto and engine heater;
battery in front
Assembly: unknown
Miscellaneous: turning circle left 10.58 m,
right 10.30 m; dry weight 1034.4 kg with
four-cylinder and 1086.5 kg with six-cylinder
engine; top speed 212 km/h
(measured on 07/13/64)
Uses: March 1964 at Reutter for series-
production preparation; July 1964 pre-series
tests; August 1964 used for holiday trip by
Ferry Porsche; 09/25/64 to 09/28/64 climate
test chamber at down to -40 °C; January 1965
suspension tests at 15 200 km; January 1965
electrical system check; 02/08/65 to 02/12/65
Wolfsburg; then body tests from 16 700 to
30 886 km (August 1965); 12/06/65 to 12/10/65
at Bilstein; total kilometer reading on 12/28/65:
50 953 km
Fate: unknown

NUMMER 10 (902/10) (912/10)

Chassis number: 13330
Color: unknown
Registration: S-UP 935 (from December 1964)
Nickname: none
Body manufactured by: Häusele
Year: 1964
Intended use: testing
Front axle: 901
Rear axle: unknown
Brakes: Teves
Engine: four-cylinder
Engine number: 830001
Transmission: 4-speed
Equipment: no door pockets, no dashboard
trim; no front bumper guards,
rubber foot mats, Goodyear tires 695-15 HE,
6 Volt electrical system
Assembly: unknown
Miscellaneous: dry weight 989 kg
Uses: in running condition 10/02/64;
December 1964 tests in Monza; early January
1965 conversion to 12 Volt system; January
18 to 22, 1965 endurance testing at 1000 km;
01/25/65 to 01/29/65 heater tests; 02/23/65
stabilizer fitted; total kilometer reading on
12/21/65: 20 100 km
Fate: sold on 10/29/65

NUMBER 11 (902/11) (912/11)

Chassis number: 13352

Color: unknown

Registration: S-UP 934 (from December 1964)

Nickname: none

Body manufactured by: Karmann in Osnabrück; delivered to Porsche on 06/29/64

Year: 1964

Intended use: unknown

Front axle: 901

Rear axle: unknown

Brakes: Teves

Engine: four-cylinder

Engine number: 813422

Transmission: first 4-speed transmission with similar ratios to 356 SC; later 5-speed transmission

Equipment: heat exchanger; 12 Volt system; three instrument dials; Goodyear tires 695-15 HE, carpets

Assembly: unknown

Miscellaneous: performance tests with 4-speed transmission on 09/17/64; tire testing on Hockenheimring (09/29/64 to 10/01/64); followed by noise measurements at 5500 km (»de-booming«); damper tests; 04/26/65 to 04/30/65 in Wolfsburg; June 1965 noise measurements at 27 500 km; 10/7 and 10/08/64 driven to Wolfsburg by Ferry Porsche; total kilometer reading on 09/27/66: 20 393 km

Fate: sold on 09/17/65

NUMBER 12 (911/12)

Chassis number: 300001

Color: Signalrot 6407 B (Signal Red)

Registration: S-UN 478 (from November 1964)

Nickname: none

Body manufactured by: Porsche; delivered 10/19/64

Year: 1964

Intended use: testing; endurance

Front axle: 901

Rear axle: 901

Brakes: Teves

Engine: 901 with dry-sump lubrication; 02/15/65 to 02/19/65 converted to roller bearings

Engine number: 121

Transmission number: 100.018-901/0

Equipment: black vinyl; Dunlop 165-15

Assembly: unknown

Uses: November 1964 pre-series tests at 4500 km; December 1964 toe-in and camber tests at 7500 km and 8300 km; 10/19 and 10/20/64 wind tunnel testing at VW plant with different tires and changes to toe-in; January 1965, Carrera engine installed; 02/08/65 to 02/12/65, tests with Carrera engine; then tests for straight-line stability at 9000 km; 03/01/65 to 03/05/65, endurance tests in Italy; 04/26/65 to 04/30/65 at Nürburgring; from 12/06/65 Girling; 12/20/65 to 12/30/65 prepared for sale; total kilometer reading on 12/28/65: 48 000 km

Fate: unknown

WHILE ONLY A FEW PICTURES OF THE PROTOTYPES EXIST, THE 901 WAS PHOTOGRAPHED MULTIPLE TIMES IN FRONT OF A VARIETY OF BACKDROPS — BELOW THE FIRST TARGA, DELIVERED TO PORSCHE AS EARLY AS 1964 BY KARMANN.

NUMBER 13 (911/13)

Chassis number: 300002

Color: Signalrot 6407 (Signal Red)

Registration: S-UN 476 (from November 1964)

Nickname: none

Body manufactured by: unknown

Year: 1964

Intended use: endurance testing

Front axle: unknown

Rear axle: unknown

Brakes: Teves

Engine: 901 with dry-sump lubrication

Engine number: 103; later four-cylinder 832060

Transmission number: 100004

Equipment: black vinyl; Dunlop 165-15;
standard Solex carburetors

Assembly: unknown

Uses: June 1964 tests at Nürburgring and in
Wolfsburg (ca. 13 000 km); November 1964
pre-series tests at 14 700 km; December 1964,
tire tests in Monza (Goodyear HE, Michelin
155 HR 15, Dunlop 165H 15 CB 57);
later endurance tests between 14 987 and
58 000 km; January 1965 training in Monte
Carlo; 02/08/65 to 02/12/65 in Wolfsburg;
05/03/65 to 05/14/65, training for the Targa
Florio; 05/17/65 to 05/21/65 at Nürburgring;
07/19/65 to 07/27/65, training for Sestrière;
08/09/65 to 08/13/65 in Wolfsburg again;
later transmission tests at 74 700 km

Fate: sold on 05/17/68

The first internal presentation to a larger audience of the »901 open car« mock-up took place on June 12, 1964 in the special build area of the bodyshell shop. Present were Ferry Porsche, his son Ferdinand Alexander, Hans Tomala, Walter Beierbach, Head of Domestic Sales Harald Wagner, Head of Bodyshell Design Erwin Komenda and Fritz Blaschka, who took the minutes. Harald Wagner once again made the case for a full convertible without a rollover bar. Finally, however, even he agreed that this would necessitate too many changes that were too expensive, such as a lower windshield and a change to the rear end of the car, let alone the safety aspects. And thus the Targa project took its course.

The first test car built by Karmann in Osnabrück and delivered to Porsche September 10, 1964 served as a visual demonstrator. Its chassis number was 13360. The decision was taken to clad the removable roof with vinyl, like the Opel Diplomat, to reduce further the width of the rollover bar and to place a shield on both sides, as on the wheel hubs, but in polished gold metallic. These shields appeared in the first sales brochure, still attached to the dark gray Targa, but never made it to series production.

On June 9, 1965, the second test car with chassis number 13396 underwent the first extensive test drive with Rolf Hannes from the Test Driving department. On August 11, 1965, Porsche finally registered the roof solution with the patent office under file reference 1455743.

Because the Targa had already been presented to the world as a safety cabriolet, the Targa test car underwent a drop test on November 10, 1965. The vehicle was lifted to a height of two meters and dropped headfirst onto a test plate. The engineers were not satisfied with the result, so the start of retail deliveries, which had been planned for early 1966, had to be postponed until January 23, 1967.

NUMBER 7 IS ALIVE

A LIVE PERFORMANCE OF THE LAST PROTOTYPE

Starting at the end of 1962, seven test cars were built en route to the series-production Porsche 901. Only one of them is known to have survived – the one with the highest evolutionary status. This is a live performance of the last prototype.

STATUS IN 1963 – ONLY TWO INSTRUMENT DIALS, AND THEY WERE DERIVED FROM THOSE OF THE BMW 503.

PAGE 149

ALL THE PARTS ALONG THE
SIDES OF THE BODYSHELL
AND THE WINDOWS DEVIATE
CONSIDERABLY FROM THE LATER
SERIES-PRODUCTION 901.

»901 from 1963/64, in need of restoration, probably the only existing 901 prototype. 20,000 dollars or highest offer.« It is September 23, 1984 when this classified ad appears in *Porsche Panorama*, the magazine published by the Porsche Club of North America. Thousands read it. But apparently nobody believes this notion that it is the last of its kind. Also unbelievable is the price expectation proffered by advertiser Paul Resnick, who operates a kind of Porsche scrap yard in New York. Well-preserved early 911s go for a third of that – and even they have very few takers.

Don Meluzio, a Chrysler dealer from Pennsylvania, knows what he wants – a one-off that will win a trophy at every classic car meet, preferably the really big one with the pretty ribbons. He loves these typically American beauty pageants; that feeling of leaving the field as the overall winner. He has also been a big Porsche fan since 1969, when he was a 21 year-old GI stationed in Butzbach, Hessen. His lieutenant drove a Porsche 912. His first sergeant took him to Hockenheim in a 911 S. It was there that he saw Porsche win almost every race. The passion took root. Don bought his first 911 in 1978. Now, as summer 1984 draws to a close, he reads the 901 ad. Is this the concours champion of his dreams?

His viewing appointment is a reality check. What Don is presented with in New York is nothing more than a rolling, dilapidated body-shell, with spray-can orange paintwork and an interior full of old parts and rat droppings. And, most importantly of all, there is absolutely no right of return should this prototype theory be disproven. Don nevertheless enters into negotiations. In the absence of any other interested parties, Resnick finally gives in at 14 500 dollars.

But this does not address the bottom line. Is the car actually one of the original 911s? Even the original 911? The chassis numbers of early series-production cars begin with three-zero-zero and have six digits. This one is 13327. There is, at this time, no literature on the history of the 911 to shed any light on this. Don writes to Porsche in 1985. He receives a brief answer, »We never issued a number 13327.« He photographs the wreck and sends the pictures to Ferdinand Alexander »Butzi« Porsche. Butzi – *Mr. Porsche Design* and father of the 911 silhouette – must surely know if the car is what it claims to be, but surely can't possibly be. Who, if

not Butzi? Don waits. Butzi does not respond. Unperturbed, the persistent collector tries again and succeeds in securing an appointment. But, when Don Meluzio arrives at Porsche Design in Zell am See on July 27, 1985, Butzi is not there – his mother Dorothea, Ferry Porsche's wife, died the previous night. Instead, the visitor from the New World is allowed to speak with employees who previously worked in Zuffenhausen. They examine the pictures and discuss the car's dubious details. Don's German is too patchy to be able to follow them. What he understands is the disparaging gestures. The conclusion drawn by the gentlemen, who try their hardest to be tactful is, »We did not build it like that.« Is Don's longed-for original an American custom car?

Back in the USA, he finds a letter from Porsche customer service in Ludwigsburg. »Enquiry received … no documentation available … forwarded to the development department.« And then comes the first ray of hope, »It could be a 911 test car.« This interim reply closes with a plea for patience – »until you hear from us again«. Finally, in January 1986, Don receives the much sought-after confirmation, »According to old

DON MELUZIO, OWNER OF THE 901 PROTOTYPE, EVEN HAD ITS FIRST LICENSE PLATES REPRODUCED.

THE SLIDING ROOF THAT OPENED FORWARD WAS THE CAUSE OF A MUCH HEATED DEBATE AT PORSCHE – AND DID NOT ENTER SERIES PRODUCTION.

drawings, this is 901 prototype number 7.« It comes with details of the car's non-series specification. At the end, Dr. Ing. h.c. F. Porsche AG wishes him every success with the restoration work. What is absent, however, it their interest in this historically significant piece – despite the fact that the company is aware of no other 901 prototype.

Don has crossed the finish line and, at the same time, is back at the start. Which parts are original? And, in any event, what does *original* actually mean in a car that was built for the purpose of ongoing change? Sensitivity is the order of the day, an understanding of the evolutionary process that once led to the 911. »We had to learn to think, feel and taste like Porsche development engineers in 1963,« says Don looking back.

By »we« he means himself and Dennis Frick, one of the best Porsche restorers in the US. Following completion of all the research, his work begins at the end of 1991. Revision of the engine is routine – the six-cylinder came from a series-production 901 from the end of 1964. But virtually everything else deviates from the later production status. The bodyshell calls for particular care and attention – only the front and rear windshields and the front bumper are the same as the later production version. But, above all, this restoration demands an unfamiliar level of perfection. The stated objective this time is not absolute flawlessness, but rather the fulfillment of the standards that Porsche set back then for its test vehicles – in line with the principle of function before aesthetics.

Accordingly, the Porsche test program overview dated July 31, 1963 stated that the production of prototype 901/7 on August 26 was to be conducted, »however, without styling refinements«. What exactly was meant by that is illustrated, for instance, by the fuel tank, which is made from countless hand-formed patch panels. The fact is that the bodyshell of the test car

WHAT IS ORIGINAL WHEN THE CURRENT STATUS WAS ONGOING CHANGE?

MAJOR COMPONENTS IN THE ENGINE COMPARTMENT, SUCH AS THE AIR FILTER AND HOOD STRUT, WERE CHANGED FOR SERIES PRODUCTION.

bearing the internal nickname Barbarossa had overall proportions that are far removed from those of the series-production version.

Consequently, the otherwise smooth line running from the upper edge of the door window to the rear window has a slight kink. And the lower bodyshell profile from the bottom edge of the window to the sill has a more rounded form similar to that of the preceding 356. The roof curvature, fenders, trunk lid – all are different from the subsequent production models. As are the side window surfaces, which are around three centimeters longer, and the doors, which are shorter in length but higher.

The most obvious differences are, of course, in the details that were completely redesigned for series production following criticism from the Testing department. Analogous historical records read today like tales of woe – records like the one composed on December 20, 1963 by Porsche development boss Helmuth Bott after he had tested the interior of the 901/7 Barbarossa. According to this, there was the risk of accidentally operating the inside door handle with the knee, and fingers were squeezed against the dashboard when winding down the right window. The most obvious of the well-over 100 features rejected during the 901 prototype phase and missing from the series-production version is Barbarossa's bizarre, forward-opening (and only half way at that) crank-operated steel sliding roof.

On the road, too, number 7 shows impressive parallels to its early development status. The car feels similar to a 911, but the setup of the pre-production suspension is somewhat evocative of the 356. Just like the sound of the engine, which exhales through two centrally positioned exhaust pipes – the solution was rejected because exhaust gas finds its way into the interior. Barbarossa is a true prototype. The last one of its kind to survive. A unique, drivable monument from the story of the creation of the greatest sports car of all time.

Don Meluzio, the pleasant and friendly man that possessed such a persistent belief in the authenticity of his over-priced purchase looks at it all far less dramatically. He simply loves sweeping up trophies – the big ones with the pretty ribbons – with his red one-off. He has 19 so far. In that respect, he is pretty relaxed about the design deficits. Just as he is, too, about the cost of the restoration, around 210 000 US dollars, because number 7 is now worth a whole lot more.

How much exactly? It is more or less impossible to put an exact figure on it. In any event, several big-name collectors asked him simply to name his price, whatever it may be. »So far, nobody has batted an eyelid at seven-figure sums,« says Don Meluzio with a laugh, immediately indicating that this is just a game for him. In fact, he stresses that, even for one million dollars plus X, Barbarossa is simply not for sale. Things were different back in 1984, as was the fact that there was only one single interested buyer back then. And the right one at that.

THE WORLD'S WEALTHIEST PORSCHE COLLECTORS OFFER RECORD SUMS FOR BARBAROSSA … IN VAIN.

REAR SKIRT STILL ONE-PIECE INSTEAD OF THREE-PIECE, TWO EXHAUST PIPES –
AND, ACCORDING TO THE STICKER ON THE PLATE, THE MAIN INSPECTION IS DUE IN 1966.

christophorus

Nr. 68/1964

chri
sto
pho
rus

Nr. 65/1963

WHAT WAS WRITTEN BACK THEN ABOUT THE 901

PRINTS OF THE ORIGINAL DRIVE REPORTS ETC.

There were just a selected few permitted to drive the 901 in 1964 – here are the opinions of those lucky journalists.

THE IMAGINATION WITH WHICH *CHRISTOPHORUS* DESIGNED ITS COVERS IN THE 1960S NEVER FAILS TO IMPRESS.

901

The new Porsche type 901 was shown for the first time in Frankfurt at the International Automobile Exhibition in September 1963. Since then Christophorus readers have sent us so many questions, that we want to answer most of them here in this 10 point list.

1. The car is called the 901 because it is the 901st Porsche design since 1931.

2. The delivery of the first cars to customers will commence in autumn 1964.

3. The 901 will be delivered with the new 6 cylinder 2 litre engine, not with the normal 356 C engine, nor with the 2 litre, 4 cylinder Carrera 2 engine.

4. For the time being the Carrera 2, because of the tremendously high demand in the past few months, will continue to be built.

5. The 901 will be equipped with a five speed gearbox, naturally with the well known Porsche patented ring synchronization.

This five speed gearbox cannot be used for the 356 C model.

6. The engine is a 6 cylinder boxer (3 cylinders opposed) with two overhead chain driven camshafts. The crankshaft (forged) has eight main bearings. The lubrication is dry sump with a scavenger and pressure pump and with an oil tank separate from the crankshaft housing. Compression ratio: 9:1. Horse power rating: 130 HP (DIN) at 6200 rpm.

7. The following performances were measured from a test car:
• top speed about 210 km/h,
• acceleration from 0 to 100 km/h in 9,1 sec,
• acceleration from 0 to 160 km/h in 21,9 sec,
• 1 kilometre from a standing start 29,9 sec,
• 400 metres from a standing start 16,4 sec,
• petrol consumption 11–14 litres for a hundred kilometres (tank capacity 68 litres).

8. The car will be equipped with braced tread tyres, size 165/15

9. The car will weigh about 1000 kilos (power to weight ratio ready to operate 7,7 kg/HP (DIN)

10. Outside dimensions: overall length 4,135 m (356 C = 4,05 m) overall width 1,60 m (1,67), overall height 1,273 m (1,31) The turning circle is exactly 10 metres (10,8).

42

Alle Jahre wieder rumorte es in der Fach- und Tagespresse des In- und Auslandes: „Porsche bringt einen großen Viersitzer!", und alle Jahre wieder mußten wir diese Meldungen dementieren— auch in diesem Jahr! Porsche brachte keinen neuen, großen viersitzigen Wagen zur Ausstellung, aber:

Seit Jahren haben sich Ferry Porsche und sein Ingenieurstab den Kopf darüber zerbrochen, wie das Porsche-Leitmotiv „Fahren in seiner schönsten Form" up-to-date gehalten und den ständig wechselnden Bedingungen des modernen Verkehrs angepaßt werden kann. Denn was heißt schon „Fahren in seiner schönsten Form?" Versteht nicht jeder von uns darunter etwas anderes? Hat nicht ein Geschäftsmann, der jeden Morgen von seinem Hause am Stadtrand in Kolonne zu seinem Büro fährt, oder die Dame, die einige Stunden später beim Shopping verzweifelt nach einem Platz an einem groschenhungrigen Parkometer sucht, ganz andere Vorstellungen vom „Fahren in seiner schönsten Form" als die kinderreiche Familie, die an die Nordsee auf Urlaub fährt, oder das glückliche junge Paar, das in einem offenen Zweisitzer auf der Autostrada del Sole mit hoher Reisegeschwindigkeit und wenig Gepäck der Sonne Süditaliens entgegenfährt? Der Geschäftsmann wird sich für sein meterweises Vorwärtskriechen sicher einen großen Amerikaner mit automatischer Kupplung wünschen; die Dame beim Parken von einem der bisher nur auf dem Papier existenten Stadtwagen träumen; der Familienvater Wert auf mindestens sechs komfortable Plätze legen und das junge Paar mit einem spartanisch ausgerüsteten Sportwagen vorlieb nehmen, wenn es sich nur den südlichen Wind bei hoher Geschwindigkeit um die Nase wehen lassen kann: dies sind nur vier Beispiele von den unzähligen Vorstellungen, die ebenso unzählige Autokäufer von dem haben, was für sie und ihre speziellen Bedürfnisse und Wünsche „Fahren in seiner schönsten Form" bedeutet.

Wie sieht es bei uns Porschefahrern aus?

Die Porsche-Ingenieure waren die ersten, die vor über 10 Jahren begannen, ein sportliches und zugleich bequemes Reisefahrzeug in größerer Serie zu bauen. Das beste Pferd im Stalle ist heute der Carrera 2000 GS; – ein Beweis dafür, daß in Zuffenhausen der einmal eingeschlagene Weg konsequent fortgesetzt

Porsche hat in den letzten Jahrzehnten viel Erfahrung im Bau und Betrieb luftgekühlter Motoren gesammelt. Ihre gute Leistung und das große Standvermögen bei den schwersten Prüfungen waren Grundlage ausgezeichneter Sporterfolge. Die bewährte Linie wurde bei der Neukonstruktion weiter verfolgt.

Luftgekühlte Motoren sind kompakt, raumsparend und leicht. Verschiedene störanfällige Bauteile der Wasserkühlung fehlen. Diese Vorzüge werden im Personenwagenbau zunehmend genutzt. Es ist erwähnenswert, daß fast 55 % aller in Deutschland erzeugten Personenwagen mit luftgekühlten Motoren ausgerüstet werden. Im Flugmotorenbau ging die Entwicklung kompromißlos zur Luftkühlung.

Die leistungsstärksten Motoren überhaupt sind heute die luftgekühlten Rennmotoren der kleinen Motorräder, die bis 200 PS pro Liter entwickeln.

Der Motorlängsschnitt zeigt bemerkenswerte Details. Die Kurbelwelle ist „vollgelagert". Das heißt: Dieser Sechszylinder-Boxermotor besitzt insgesamt acht Kurbelwellenlager (je eines zwischen jedem Zylinder, je eines an den beiden Enden des Motors und ein zusätzliches am Antrieb für Lichtmaschine und Gebläse). Zwei Ölpumpen sorgen für den Schmierkreislauf. Die eine saugt das Öl aus dem Trockensumpf ab, die andere fördert aus dem vom Motor getrennten Behälter zu den Lagerstellen. Es ist ein Axialgebläserad verwendet, das auf der Welle der Wechselstrom-Lichtmaschine sitzt und durch einen Keilriemen angetrieben wird. Die sechs Vergaser sind an ein Trockenluftfilter mit Papierpatrone angeschlossen. Rechts unten im Kurbelgehäuse sind zwei Kettenräder zu erkennen, die je eine Nockenwelle pro Motorseite antreiben. Das Einzelhubvolumen pro Zylinder beträgt

nur 333 ccm: mit eine Grundlage für die Drehzahl- und Leistungssteigerung.

Die Vollagerung der Kurbelwelle ist bei Boxermotoren dieser Größe ungewöhnlich, doch ein sicheres Mittel gegen zu hohe Biegebeanspruchung. Im Laufe der Zeit sind die Triebwerkbelastungen ja ganz allgemein sehr stark gewachsen. Mit der Verdichtung zum Beispiel wurden die Zünddrücke wesentlich höher. Verstärkt wird ihre Wirkung durch die Tendenz zu großen Bohrungen und kleinen Hüben, wobei die größeren Bohrungen zusätzlich größere Lagerabstände und Biegelängen zur Folge haben. Durch Steigerung der Drehzahlen sind in ähnlicher Weise auch die Massenkräfte größer geworden. Die Vollagerung – im Dieselmotor allgemein verwendet – war ein Mittel, dem zu begegnen. Gleichzeitig ist auch dem Werkstoffsektor und besonders durch entsprechende Wärmebehand-

lung (z. B. das Tenifer-Verfahren) viel erreicht worden.

Der Motor des 901 hat pro Seite je eine obenliegende Nockenwelle. Sie werden über ein Zwischenrad und je eine Kette von der Kurbelwelle angetrieben. Der Kettenantrieb besitzt ein Spannrad, es wird ölhydraulisch angedrückt. Drei Führungsschienen mit Gummibelag hindern die Kette am Schwingen. Die Ein- und Auslaßventile sind V-förmig zueinander gestellt. Sie werden über Kipphebel betätigt. Der Brennraum ist halbkugelig ausgebildet, mit glatter und kleiner wärmeaufnehmender Fläche.

Am Einlaß ist ein großvolumiger Trockenluftfilter den Vergasern vorgeschaltet. Die Auspuffanlage besteht aus einem Sammelrohr je Seite, in das drei Auslaßkanäle einmünden und das die Gase in einen „Vortopf" leitet. Von dort führt ein Rohr zum hinten liegenden Abgasschalldämpfer.

Das Leistungsdiagramm der verschiedenen Motoren zeigt, daß C und SC bis zu 4000 Touren ungefähr die gleiche Leistung haben, die PS des SC kommen erst „oben" voll zur Geltung. Der 901 dagegen hat durch sein besseres Drehmoment schon ab 2500 Touren eine erheblich bessere Leistung, die bis 5000 U/min fast so gut ist wie die des 904 mit der normalen, nicht für Höchstdrehzahlen ausgelegten Serien-Auspuffanlage. — Mit dem Rennauspuff ist der 904 konkurrenzlos

The performance chart of the various engines shows that the C and SC have about the same performance up to 4.000 rpm, and the HP of the SC really comes into it's own at the upper end

Ce diagramme des puissances des différents moteurs montre que C et SC ont, jusqu'à 4.000 tours, à peu près la même puissance. Par contre, le 901, grâce à son meilleur moment de rotation, atteint dès 2.500 tours une puissance bien plus forte qui, à 5.000 t/m, égale presque celle du 904 avec échappement de série normal et non pas étudié pour nombre de tours maximum. Avec échappement pour courses, la 904 est sans concurrent

Rechts: Motor-Querschnitt. Man erkennt oben das Gebläse, links darunter den Verteiler. Die beiden obenliegenden Nockenwellen (rechts und links außen) werden durch eine Kette angetrieben, die (rechts im Bild deutlich zu sehen) durch ein eigenes Zwischenrad mit einem automatisch arbeitenden Druckventil immer in der richtigen Spannung gehalten wird

Right: Engine cross-section. One can see the fan at the top, and below it on the left the distributor. The two overhead camshafts (right and left outer) are driven by a chain which is easily noticeable on the right of the picture and which is held at the correct tension by a pressure valve which works automatically

A droite: coupe de moteur. On reconnaît au dessus le compresseur, à gauche au-dessous le distributeur. Les deux arbres à cames en tête (à l'extérieur droit et gauche) seront entraînés par une chaine qui, (nettement visible à droite de la photo) grâce à une roue intermédiaire avec soupape de compression fonctionnant automatiquement est maintenue dans la tension adéquate

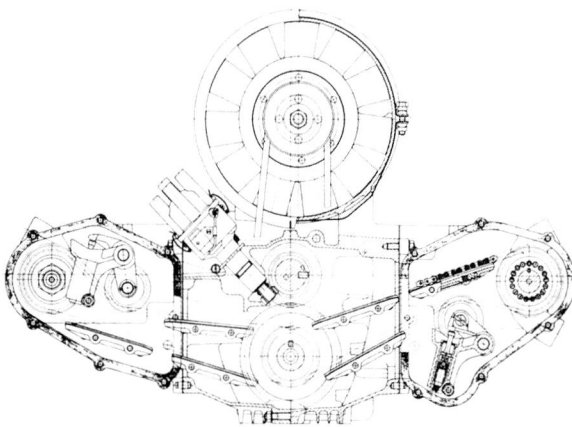

PORSCHE
PANORAMA

OCTOBER 1963   Vol. VIII, No. 10

PRODUCTION SLATED FOR 1964

Porsche announces new Type 901

The long-rumored 6-cylinder 2 liter Porsche engine powering the new Type 901 car was announced by the Porsche factory late in August.

In a voluminous but vague announcement the new car was said to be not a 4 seater but a 2 + 2. On the cover, below, and on page 4 you will find all available photos sent to PANORAMA. Pictures of the engine evidently are not available.

Following are excerpts from the Factory's announcement, with some of the subjectiveness and translation peculiarities edited out:

Body and chassis

The body is even more aerodynamically smooth in form than the 356 Type. By increasing the wheelbase 120mm it became possible to enlarge the seating area, especially in the rear.

The overall width was reduced by 70mm, an advantage in today's traffic. In addition, the previous inside width has not only been retained but has been increased. The doors have been designed in such a manner that their greater width enables passengers to get in and out of the rear seats with greater ease.

The front fenders are fastened to the body by screws to facilitate front-end repair. The ventilation has been improved.

Engine

An opposed, 6 cylinder, air-cooled 2 liter engine is used since it is possible to reach higher RPM, and therefore higher power more economically than with a 4 cylinder engine. Both the Grand Prix and sports car experience were put to use in the design of this engine which has 1 overhead cam per cylinder bank. The cams, for the first time at Porsche, are driven by double row roller chains, while the forged crankshaft has 8 main bearings.

Transmission, axle, steering

A new 5-speed transmission was designed for this new engine.

The front suspension unit consists of a lower wishbone and shock absorber while the springing action is taken up by longitudinal torsion bars.

The rear suspension has trailing links which are supported by means of transverse torsion bars.

The rack and pinion steering is set up in the middle of the car. The steering column is divided

---

by means of 2 universal joints and does not run straight through, thus eliminating the possibility of the steering column being pushed through into the driver's seat.

All 4 wheels are equipped with disc brakes.

Price was not announced.

TECHNICAL DATA

ENGINE

Type	flat 6, 3 cylinders on each side, air-cooled
Bore	80mm
Stroke	66mm
Displacement	1991 cc
Compression ratio	9:1
Bhp (DIN) at 6200	130 hp (approx), 150 SAE
Torque max.	16.5 mkg at 4600 rpm
Top speed	120 mph

CHASSIS

Front suspension	lower wishbone and shock absorber wheel support unit (ball joints)
Front springs	longitudinal torsion bars
Rear suspension	trailing links
Rear springs	transverse torsion bars
Anti-roll bar	front and rear

STEERING — rack and pinion

DIMENSIONS

Wheelbase	2204 mm
Track, front	1332 mm
Track, rear	1312 mm
Overall length	4135 mm
Body width	1600 mm
Height	1320 mm
Turning circle	10 meters
Fuel tank	74 liters

REGIONAL NEWS

'This is PCA' project under way by Cascade Region

Bernie L. Freemesser, President of the Cascade Region, says that many more Regions must respond to the request made in the July issue of PANORAMA (p 13) to make the proposed color slide show a success.

This will be a set of slides with the narration on tape. Sets will be available on loan from the PCA Executive Office. This project was authorized by the Board at its meeting during the 7th Parade.

Each Region should submit 6 to 8 35mm color slides of their Region—its activities, its racing, and its scenery. Send along a written script describing the slides.

Freemesser told PANORAMA: "What we are trying to do is not show 150 slides of people standing in front of Porsches, but rather a complete picture of each Region so that when it's shown at a meeting the viewer will feel that he is a part of a national organization. A slide with scenery to introduce the Region is vital because that is the major difference in the Regions. We also need some good action shots of members racing or the like, plus unusual activity pictures."

Freemesser wants to receive all slides from all Regions by Nov. 15 so that the project will be ready for distribution during early 1964. Send slides to: B. L. Freemesser, 3241 Donald Street, Eugene, Oregon.

PORSCHE
PANORAMA

DECEMBER 1964   Vol. IX, No. 12

NIC MATTLINGER OF POAC REPORTS

More on the 901, 904, 906, 911

Nic Mattlinger, Assistant General Service Manager, Porsche of America Corporation, Teaneck, N.J, spoke recently before the Hudson-Champlain Region at a dinner meeting. Because his comments are of interest to all POAC members, we are presenting them here in edited form and paraphrased where necessary to make the meaning clear and the reading more rapid.

The Porsche of America Corporation, as you know, was for many years a nation-wide organization that served only as liaison between the Factory, and dealers and distributors in the United States. We have 7 distributors in the United States who also act as importers.

One of the distributors in the east for many years was Hoffman Motors Corp., New York City. On May 1, 1964, POAC took over the Hoffman territory in 11 eastern states. So now, as some people like to say, POAC wears 2 hats, 1 as a distributor, and 1 as a nationwide factory liaison organization.

One main result of this change was that we now have in Teaneck a parts department for the entire 11-state area. The parts business has increased 52% since we took it over from Hoffman.

In Teaneck we have a nationwide parts department for all Porsche competition drivers. We try to help competition drivers because they do a lot of 'advertising' for us. They get parts with a 20% discount if they drive the 1600 Normal, Super, or Super 90. If they drive a Type 904, or a Spyder, they get parts at our cost. In this way we help them and make it easier for them to afford to race.

The building itself in Teaneck contains 10,000 square feet and we have a total parts inventory of $220,000.

As you read in PANORAMA some time ago, the Factory took over the Reutter body plant. We bought this plant and we have about 3500 employees instead of the 12 or 13 hundred employees we had. Actually, it is not a Reutter body anymore, it is a Porsche body. Also, Karmann makes about 25 Porsche bodies a day.

Production is running at the rate of about 50

cars a day and it will stay that way. We have no room to increase it any further.

The new Type 901 has aroused interest in this country and I would like to tell you some further information about it. Every distributor in the United States is getting one 901 the latter part of November. This car will be driven only by Porsche service personnel because we want to drive this car really hard and find out if we will have any problems with it in this country. Actually, the speed limit in the United States sometimes causes car problems because they can't be driven any faster than 60 miles an hour, or sometimes even 55 mph.

These new 901's with each distributor will be driven hard, especially during the winter. Then they will be taken apart to determine any further facts about the car. We will let the Factory know right away when we find out.

I have here a newspaper writeup reporting on the

Nic Mattlinger of POAC

Porsche 901 mit Sechszylindermotor

Ein völlig neues Modell mit 6-Zylinder-Boxermotor von 130 PS — Fünfganggetriebe — Neue Karosserielinie

Der ersten Ankündigung des neuen Modelljahres bei Porsche mit dem rationalisierten Typenprogramm aber unveränderter Karosserie folgt soeben eine zweite, weit bedeutsamere, welche ganz erhebliche Aenderungen in der Konzeption mit sich bringt. Neben den in «AR» 36 beschriebenen Typen 365 C mit den Motoren 1600 C (früher S 75) und 1600 CS (früher S 90) tritt als Neuheit das Modell 901, dessen Produktion erst in geraumer Zeit beginnen wird.

Die Hauptmerkmale des 901 sind der *wiederum* im Heck untergebrachte kompakte, luftgekühlte Sechszylinder-Boxermotor von 1991 cm^3 Inhalt und 130 PS Leistung, ein vollsynchronisiertes Getriebe mit fünf Gängen, eine neue Vorderradaufhängung mit Querlenkern und Längs-

PORSCHE 901 IN NEUER KAROSSERIEFORM — Die neue Karosserie weist wiederum 2 + 2 Plätze auf. Sie ist trotz der vergrösserten Fenster und der eckigeren Konturen strömungsgünstiger als jene der Modelle 365. (Photo Dr. Seifert)

torsionsstäben, und eine neue Coupé-Karosserie mit zwei Plätzen und zwei Notsitzen.

Der Neukonstruktion lag die Idee zugrunde, ein Reisefahrzeug zu schaffen, das auch im dichten Verkehr angenehm gehandhabt werden kann, im übrigen aber in den Fahrleistungen dem Carrera nicht nachsteht. In der Tat stimmen die Leistungsdaten des Sechszylindermotors mit denjenigen des durch seine grosse Elastizität berühmt gewordenen Zweiliter-Viernockenwellenmotors überein.

Der neue Sechszylinder

Die Wahl eines Sechszylinders wird von Porsche damit begründet, dass er gegenüber dem Vierzylinder den Vorteil einer höheren Drehzahlgrenze habe und dass seine Fertigung wirtschaftlich noch tragbar sei. Der neue Boxermotor hat Zylinderabmessungen von 80 mm Bohrung und nur 66 mm Hub, er ist somit noch kurzhubiger als alle frühern Porschemotoren. Bei der gleichen Nenndrehzahl für die Höchstleistung von 6600 U/min beträgt die mittlere Kolbengeschwindigkeit beim neuen Motor nur noch 1,36 m/sec gegenüber 2,96 m/sec. Wie beim 1600 SC beträgt auch beim neuen 901 die Verdichtung 9 : 1. Das höchste Drehmoment wird bei 4600 U/min mit 16,5 mkg abgegeben. Die Maximalleistung beträgt 130 DIN-PS bei 6200 U/min.

Während *Porsche bis anhin immer* entweder Stossstangen oder vier obenliegende Nockenwellen (Carrera) für die Ventilbetätigung anwandte, findet man beim neuen Sechszylinder nunmehr je eine Nockenwelle pro Zylinderblock, die nicht über Zahnräder, sondern über Ketten angetrieben wird. Die Kurbelwelle des Sechszylinders ist achtmal gelagert.

Ueber jeder Zylinderreihe sind je zwei Doppelvergaser angeordnet, deren Saugrohre in einen sehr flachen, breiten gemeinsamen Luftfilter münden. Die Kühlluft wird durch ein hochliegendes Radialgebläse gefördert.

Kraftübertragung und Radaufhängung

Zu den grossen Neuerungen gehört ferner ein vollsynchronisiertes Fünfganggetriebe. Der Motor liegt wiederum hinter der Achse, er treibt das Getriebe durch das Hinterachsgehäuse hindurch an. Die Antriebswellen weisen Doppelgelenke auf.

Eine wesentliche Abkehr von der bisherigen, ursprünglich vom VW *übernommenen* Bauart *zeigt sich* an der Vorderradaufhängung, wo man nunmehr zu untern Querlenkern mit

NEUE PROPORTIONEN — Der Radstand ist gegenüber dem Modell 365 um 12 cm länger und beträgt nun 220,4 cm, die Gesamtbreite ist mit 16 cm um 7 cm schmäler, trotzdem ist der Innenraum grösser und der Einstieg bequemer Ueber dem Heckfenster sind Entlüftungsschlitze angebracht.

PORSCHE SECHSZYLINDER-2-LITER-MOTOR — Der kurzhubige Sechszylinder mit gegenüberliegenden Zylindern leistet 130 PS. Pro Zylinderblock ist eine Nockenwelle mit Kettenantrieb vorhanden. (Werkbild)

PORSCHE 911 — Seit der ersten Präsentation des Prototyps 1963 wurde die Typenbezeichnung 901 auf 911 geändert, und zudem hat der Serienwagen in seiner heutigen Form noch zahlreiche Aenderungen erfahren, die ihm den Charakter eines schnellen, komfortablen und geräumigeren Coupés geben. (Photos B. Cahier)

Porsche 911 aus der Serie

Aenderung der Typenbezeichnung von 901 auf 911 — Serienfabrikation hat begonnen
Zahlreiche Aenderungen gegenüber dem Prototyp 1963

Den mit Spannung erwarteten neuen Porsche mit der damaligen Typenbezeichnung 901 bekam die Weltöffentlichkeit erstmals an der *Frankfurter Automobilausstellung 1963* in

Drei Kurzteste enthüllen drei verschiedene Fahrzeugtypen

Die drei sportlichen Fahrzeuge, welche den Gegenstand dieser Kurzteste von Bernhard Cahier bilden, haben das Publikumsinteresse durch ihre überragenden Fahrleistungen und ihr sportliches Renommé auf sich gezogen. Der Porsche 911 (ehemals 901) gehört zur Gruppe der komfortablen und schnellen GT. Im Renault R8 Gordini erkennt man ein Fahrzeug, das der Grossserie nahe verwandt ist, durch Gordinis Frisiermassnahmen jedoch mit englischen und italienischen Derivationen in Konkurrenz tritt. Mit dem Ford Mustang «Tour de France» wurde ein Einzelexemplar dem Kurztest unterworfen, das als Siegerwagen wesentlich von der Serienausführung, wie sie jetzt auch in der Schweiz vertreten ist, abweicht. Red.

der Form eines mit allen Promessen des Prototyps behafteten Ausstellungsstars zu sehen. Wenn auch die damals genannten Preise noch zu hoch erschienen, die Innenausstattung wenig attraktiv war und die gelbe Farbe für dieses Coupé schlecht gewählt war, so wirkte die Neuerscheinung nach so vielen Jahren der Kontinuität dennoch sensationell. Porsche konnte schon auf Grund dieses Prototyps dank dem von unzähligen Sporterfolgen untermauerten Renommé bereits zahlreiche Bestellungen notieren. Die Mise-au-point für den Serienanlauf hat dann bekanntlich viel Zeit in Anspruch genommen; die Anhänger der Marke wurden auf eine harte Probe gestellt. Das Produktionsdatum Frühjahr 1964 verstrich ohne sichtbaren Erfolg. Das Erscheinen des neuen Modells wurde alsdann auf den September angekündigt. Tatsächlich fand dann auch die Belieferung der Vertretungen mit den ersten Wagen statt. In den letzten Monaten dieses Jahres kam die Serienproduktion in Gang.

Gleichzeitig ereignete sich etwas Seltsames. Die *Typenbezeichnung* wurde von 901 auf 911 geändert, ohne dass damit eine konstruktive Aenderung an den Fahrzeugen verbunden gewesen wäre. Der Grund lag einzig darin, dass eine französische Firma die Null an zweiter Stelle einer dreistelligen Typenbezeichnung der Firma Porsche auf der Ebene des Markenrechts streitig machte, worauf sich Porsche zur Aenderung auf 911 bereitfand.

Nach neuester Information durch den Leiter der Sportabteilung, Huschke von Hanstein, wurde vor einigen Wochen die *Produktionszahl* 100 bereits überschritten und die Wagen ausgeliefert, so dass nun die Homologation bei der FIA-Behörde nachgesucht wird. Für den *schweizerischen Markt* teilte uns der Generalimporteur mit, dass noch mit Lieferfristen von 4 bis 6 Monaten zu rechnen sei und dass der Preis auf Fr. 29 750.— festgesetzt wurde.

Neuer Wagen in Porsche-Tradition

Die seit der Frankfurter Ausstellung verstrichene zweite Entwicklungsphase, welche vom Prototyp zum Serienfahrzeug führte, rechtfertigt es, die technischen Spezifikationen des 911 kurz zu resumieren. Wie alle Porsche-Fahrzeuge, besitzt auch der 911 einen *Heckmotor*, der in der Fahrzeuglängsachse im hintern Ueberhang eingebaut ist. Es handelt sich dabei um einen neuen, wie immer luftgekühlten *Sechszylinder* mit je drei gegenüberliegenden waagrechten Zylindern, mit je einer obenliegenden Nockenwelle pro Block. Aus einem Hub von 66 mm und einer Bohrung von 80 mm resultiert ein Inhalt von 1991 cm^3. Bei einer Verdichtung von 9 : 1 beträgt die Leistung 130 DIN-PS (bzw. 150 SAE-PS) bei 6100 U/min. Das höchste Drehmoment von 18 mkg wird bei 4200 U/min erreicht. Die Gemischversorgung erfolgt durch zwei Solex-Spezialvergaser mit drei Lufttrichtern.

Die Karosserie weicht stark und vorteilhaft von der Linie des 356 ab. Die stark bombierten Formen sind härteren Linienzügen, schärferen Konturen und geglätteten Flächen gewichen. Dank dem von 207 auf 230 cm verlängerten Radstand ist der Innenraum grösser, und der Wagen reiht sich nun in die echten 2 + 2-Coupés mit zwei brauchbaren hintern Sitzen ein. In der Gesamtlänge übertrifft der 911 das Modell 365 nur um 2,5 cm, in der Breite um 13 cm, während die Gesamthöhe mit 132 cm unverändert geblieben ist.

Das Interieur des Prototyps ist für die Serie völlig neu gestaltet worden und zeigt nun attraktivere Züge. Am Instrumentenbrett, das mit Holzfournier verkleidet und mit Polsterung versehen ist, sind die Instrumente funktionell richtig angeordnet. Die Einzelsitze sind mit einer Kombination aus Leder und Stoff bezogen, zweckmässig geformt, regulierbar und für Langstreckenfahrten komfortabel. Das Lenkrad weist in der Originalausführung einen Holzring auf. An einer Konsole an der Lenksäule sind die Schalter für den Scheibenwischer, die Blinker und die Scheinwerfer angeordnet. Das Fünfganggetriebe durch einen kurzen Mittelschalt bedient.

Die gegenüber dem Modell 365 sentlich vergrösserten und vor höheren Fenster ergeben eine b

(Fortsetzung Se

Porsche 911

Fahrleistungen

Beschleunigung	
0— 80 km/h	6
0—100 km/h	8
0—130 km/h	15,
0—160 km/h	24,
Stehender Kilometer	
400 m	16
1000 m	29,
Höchstgeschwindigkeit	
(im Kurztest) 209 km/h	

NEUES ARMATURENBRETT — Die Instrumente sind vor dem Lenkrad angeordnet, und das Armaturenbrett mit Holzfournier ist mit Lederpolstern versehen.

BRAUCHBARER KOFFERRAUM — Im Vergleich zum Modell 365 verfügt der Porsche 911 über einen langen, breiten Kofferraum.

HINTERSITZE MIT KLAPPLEHNEN — Die neuen beiden hintern Einzelsitze mit Klapplehnen machen den Porsche 911 zu einem echten Coupé mit 2+2 Sitzen.

150 SAE-PS AUF KLEINEM RAUM — Der luftgekühlte Sechszylinder-Boxermotor im hintern Karosserieüberhang leistet jetzt 150 SAE-PS bei 6100 U/min.

RENAULT R 8 GORDINI — Zwei weisse Streifen über der linken Karosserieseite und das renn liche französische Blau sowie eine tieferliegende Karosserie kennzeichnen äusserlich den auf frisierten R 8 Gordini, der seine Feuertaufe im Korsika-Rallye erhalten hat.

Der R8-Gordini von Renault

Von Gordini hochgezüchteter R 8 Major mit 95 PS Leistung
Aenderungen an der Hinterradaufhängung ergeben neutrales Kurvenverhalten

Renault ist in Frankreich das zurzeit am stärksten am Automobilsport interessierte Werk. Seine Aktivität beruht zu einem schönen Teil aus den engen Verbindungen zu *Amédé Gordini;* sie erstreckte sich im übrigen auf die Tourenwagen, GT- und Rennwagenkategorie wie auch auf die gelegentlich auftauchenden Prototypen. Auf dem Sportwagenmarkt spielt die Marke auch als Motorenlieferant für die Konstruktionen von Jean Rédélé und René Bonnet eine wichtige Rolle.

Unter eigener Marke erschienen in den letzten Jahren auf dem Sportsektor der Reihe nach der 4 CV «1063», dann der Renault Dauphine Gordini und sodann der Dauphine «1093», dem in jüngster Zeit als sportliche Version des R 8 der von unserem Mitarbeiter gefahrene R 8 Gordini folgte. In Frankreich wurde dieses hochgezüchtete Sportfahrzeug schon lange erwartet, da im Kampf gegen die *Mini Cooper* und die kleinen *Abarth* eine entsprechende Waffe fehlte. Der neue R 8 Gordini debütierte an der anspruchsvollen *Tour de Corse* (Korsika-Rallye) mit Glanz; sie belegten den ersten, dritten, vierten und fünften Platz.

Der R 8 Gordini wurde erstmals am Pariser Autosalon der breiten Oeffentlichkeit gezeigt. Das kleine Wägelchen kündigte schon durch die hellblaue Farbe, als Symbol für französische Sportfahrzeuge, seine rennsportlichen Ambitionen an, es trägt als Modellbezeichnung den Namen Gordini und weist damit auf die grossen Verdienste dieses Konstrukteurs um die aktive Beteiligung Frankreichs am Autosport hin.

Hohe Motorleistung und angepasste Radaufhängung

Aeusserlich bewahrt der R 8 Gordini das Gesicht des Serienwagens, von dem er abgeleitet ist. Hinweise auf die Sonderausführungen sind durch die blaue Farbe und die weissen Stre an der Karosserie gegeben. Bei nauerer Betrachtung erkennt dass der Wagen tiefer liegt als die nault-Serienmodelle R 8.

Der Motor und die Aufhäng wurden einer gründlichen Revision terzogen. Sie sind detailliert in « 41 beschrieben. Wir erinnern hier an, dass Gordini die Leistung des Motors von 45 auf 95 SAE-PS aufgeschraubt hat. Die Leistungss gerung wurde vor allem durch Verwendung eines von Gordini wickelten *Zylinderkopfs* aus Stahl halbkugelförmigen *Brennräumen* in V-Form angeordneten *Ventilen* reicht, die jedoch wie beim Ser motor durch eine seitliche Nock welle, diese jedoch mit *speziellen* N kenformen, betätigt werden. Der halt beträgt 1108 cm^3 (stimmt mit d jenigen des Serienmotors R 8 M überein). An die Stelle des Einf vergasers treten zwei Solex-*Dop körpervergaser*. Die Kompression w de auf 10,4 : 1 erhöht. Mit dieser A rüstung entwickelt der fünffach lagerte Motor seine Höchstleistung 6500 U/min.

Die Hinterradaufhängung best aus Pendelachsen und Schraub federn mit insgesamt vier Stossdä fern. Die Schraubenfedern sind v und hinten verkürzt, und dadu kommt der Schwerpunkt des Wag tiefer zu liegen. Die Lenkung arbe direkter als beim Serienmodell, die vom R 8 übernommenen vier Sc benbremsen wurden mit einer Ser hilfe vervollständigt.

Angenehme Sitzposition

Die für ihren Komfort und ihren ten Seitenhalt bekannten Sitze des rienmodells R 8 wurden unveränd in das Sportfahrzeug übernomm

(Fortsetzung Seite

sfreudige Frankfurter ›ilausstellung

; von Seite 17)

PS gehoben, was nebenbei die Verwendung von Super- ›twendig macht. Beim Modell st die Leistung um 5 PS auf stiegen, ein Gewinn der mit rdichtung von 8,6 : 1 und euen Solex-Registervergaser vurde. Im gleichen Sinne ist l verfahren, wo die Leistung m Rekord L und im Rekord erwendeten Motoren von 63 S und im Kadett Coupé von 3 PS angestiegen ist. Dieser Motor wird bald auch im Kadett und im Station- stalliert werden. Der Zug zur ung in der Mittelklasse esen Herbst von VW ange- der 1,5-Liter mit Zweiver- srüstung und einer auf 8,5: 1 ten Verdichtung sowie höhe- zahl mit 54 statt 45 PS her- ı. Auch der Porsche-Motor ist um 5 PS auf 95 PS gestie-

Leistungsänderungen haben bestehenden Modellen die on bei Coupé und Roadster die Marke BMW bei den Mo- 500 und der Serie 3200, der Ford Taunus 12 M mit 1,2- tor, alle Modelle von Glas ter Inhalt mit Einschluss des chen Goggomobils, alle seit herausgekommenen Merce- -Typen, die NSU-Prinzen Sport, die Grundmodelle lett, Rekord 1,5 und 1,7 Liter, die Porsche-Modelle 356 C Leistung von 75 PS bei 5200 att 5000 U/min) sowie der VW 1500 (ohne S).

remsen im Vormarsch

utsche Automobilindustrie ist ıtiv kurzer Bedenkzeit zur gen Verwendung der Schei- se übergegangen. Ein beson- rkmal, das an der IAA zum Vor- am, ist die nunmehr serien- Ausrüstung, die der früheren usführung gegen Mehrpreis n ist. VW bleibt bei allen Mo- er Trommelbremse treu, fer- den der DKW F 11, der BMW Ford Taunus 12 M und TS, ggomobil und die Glas-Isar- der NSU Prinz IV und der inz sowie der Opel Kadett ässig mit Trommelbremse ver- Die ATE-Scheibenbremse, Li- nlop, hat sich als Unterliefe- deutschen Fahrzeughersteller h eine Monopolstellung er- was natürlich für den Brem- ce innerhalb Deutschlands sster Bedeutung ist. Die Liste ATE-Scheibenbremsen serien- oder auf Wunsch versehenen n Marken umfasst 31 Typen. rt zu den wichtigsten Neue- des Mercedes-Programms, dass nunmehr jeder Personenwagen serienmässig mit einem Zweikreis-Servobremssystem mit Scheibenbremsen vorn und ab Typ 300 SE an allen Rädern ausgerüstet wird. Auf dem Deutschen Markt bedingte dies eine Preiserhöhung um 160 DM bei den Modellen 190, 190 D und 220. Von Bedeutung ist auch, dass nunmehr die Modelle von Glas aus der Reihe 1004 und 1204 auf Wunsch mit Scheibenbremsen verbessert werden können. Die beiden neuen Modelle 1500 und 1300 GT sind damit serienmässig ausgerüstet. Neu ist auch, dass nunmehr Vorderradscheibenbremsen bei allen Ford-17M-Modellen zur Normalausrüstung gehören. Eine Besonderheit bietet der grosse Mercedes 600, der an den Vorderrädern je zwei Bremszangen besitzt.

M DEN NEUEN GLAS 1300 GT — Oben ›ler-Motor mit 75 DIN-PS, obenliegen- ›kenwelle, Solex-Doppelvergaser und gelagerter Kurbelwelle. (Werkbild)

ie mit geripptem Stoff überzogenen, n Einzelsessel mit seitlichen Stütz- (Photo Seifert)

Variantenreiche Aufhängungssysteme

Der deutsche Markt bietet fast ebensoviele Aufhängungsarten an Vorder- und Hinterrädern wie Modelle, die Standardform mit vorderen Dreieckquerlenkern und Schraubenfedern sowie hinterer Starrachse und Blattfeder ist praktisch nur noch beim Opel Rekord und Ford 17 M, sonst aber nirgends mehr in Reinkultur erhalten geblieben. Die vielen Wagen mit Front- und Heckmotoren sorgen ohnehin für Abwechslung in den Aufhängungssystemen. Man sieht aber an dieser grossen Vielfalt, mit wieviel Eifer die deutschen Ingenieure den Problemen des sicheren und komfortablen Fahrverhaltens auf den Leib rükken und wieviel Freude sie an originellen Lösungen haben. Wir erinnern in diesem Zusammenhang an die Hinterradführung beim Opel Kadett mit dem kurzen Schubrohr, an die Marke DKW, die für jeden der drei Haupttypen eine eigene Vorder- und Hinterradaufhängung als Optimum herausfand, die immer wieder neue Abarten der vordern Einzelradaufhängung und der hinteren Starrachse darstellen. Unverändert ist die Eingelenkpendelachse mit tiefliegendem Drehpunkt bei allen Mercedes-Typen, somit auch beim Grossen Mercedes 600, wo sie das basse Erstaunen der Cadillac- und Rolls-Royce-Ingenieure herausfordern dürfte.

Neue Wege hat auch Porsche beim für eine spätere Zeit vorgesehenen Prototyp 901 in der Vorder- und Hinterradaufhängung eingeschlagen. Der neue Porsche 901 verfolgt die Linie des zu höchst sportlichen Fahrleistungen befähigten, aber auch komfortablen Reisewagens, und demzufolge mussten auch bei der Konstruktion des Fahrwerkes manche Kompromisse geschlossen werden, die neben allen sportlichen Eigenschaften auch durch eine angenehm empfundene Federung und einen grossen vorderen Kofferraum diktiert wurden.

Auf der Suche nach einer raumsparenden Vorderradaufhängung mit langen Federwegen hat man die Kurbelachse mit Quertorsionsstäben verlassen und die Räder an unteren Führungsarmen mit Längstorsionsstäben und nach oben an einer dem McPherson-Federbein ähnlichen Konstruktion geführt. In diesen Federbeinen sind die Stossdämpfer eingebaut. An den Hinterrädern wurde die Pendelachse verlassen und durch eine positive Radführung mit Dreiecklenker und Längslenkerarm, an dem die Torsionsstabfeder (quer) angreift, ersetzt. Die Räder werden je über eine Doppelgelenkwelle angetrieben. Die gegenüber einer Pendelachse bei dieser Radaufhängung weit geringeren Abweichungen in der Spur und im Radsturz verringern die Uebersteuerungstendenz.

Eine normale Starrachse mit Längsblattfederung und Gummihohlkörpern, jedoch ohne zusätzliche Führungselemente, besitzen die neuen Modelle von Glas, der 1500 und der 1300 GT.

Der Zug zum Coupé

Es entspricht zweifellos den Bedürfnissen des Marktes, wenn zugleich oder etwas später mit dem Erscheinen eines neuen Normalmodelles die Station-Wagon-Karosserien lanciert werden, wie dies bei VW, Opel und Ford geschehen ist. Mit der IAA zielen sowohl Ford wie Opel auf die Liebhaber einer preisgünstigen Coupékarosserie hin. Beide Marken verwenden dazu bis zur Höhe der Gürtellinie die Rohkarosserie der zweitürigen Modelle. Die Coupékarosserie ist eine exklusive Erscheinung, deren Eleganz und Linienführung durch die Kreationen der Spezialkarossiers auf ein sehr hohes ästhetisches Niveau gebracht wurden. Es darf daher nicht verwundern, dass die Auto Union, Mercedes, Ghia-Karmann, NSU für ihre eleganten und bestechend ins Auge fallende Coupéausführungen von Kopf bis Fuss von den Normalmodellen abweichende Formen gewählt haben. Nicht so Ford und Opel, welche gerade die Geräumigkeit ihrer zweitürigen Coachs zum Vorwand nehmen, auf diesen Grundformen ein Coupédach aufzusetzen. Der Gesamteindruck hängt dann, wie die neuen Realisationen zeigen, sehr stark von den Proportionen des Unterteils ab, er wird vor allem mitbestimmt durch die Karosseriehöhe über den Radkasten vorn und hinten.

Die Kölner Fordwerke enthüllten an der IAA ein neues Coupé auf der Grundkarosserie des 12 M mit dem 1,5-Liter-TS-Motor von 55 PS. Durch die elegant hingelegte Dachlinie, die hohe, mit Chromrahmen eingefasste bombierte Windschutzscheibe und das ins Dach hineingezogene Heckfenster macht dieses, auch leistungsmässig etwas Besonderes bietendes Modell, einen sehr ansprechenden Eindruck. Das Fahrzeug enthält natürlich noch durch den Frontantrieb und den V4-Zylindermotor seine individuelle Note.

Die Firma Opel hat auf die Ausstellung hin gleich zwei neue Coupés ins Feld geschickt, die auf den Modellen Kadett und auf dem zweitürigen Rekord aufgebaut werden. Beim Rekord steht das viersitzige Coupé in guter Harmonie zu dem als sehr schick und im verjüngten amerikanischen Stil empfundenen Grundaufbau. Das Dach ist leicht und das kleine hintere Seitenfenster besonders geformt. Die Ausstattung des mit einer breiten und durch eine abklappbare Mittelarmlehne getrennten hinteren Sitzbank versehenen Innenraums zeigt die Komfortmerkmale des Luxusmodells der Rekord-Reihe, beispielsweise Liegesitze. Die Motorenleistung liegt beim Coupé mit 67 DIN-PS etwa um 10 PS über derjenigen des Normalmodelles. Das Vierganggetriebe wird durch einen Mittelschalthebel bedient, und Scheibenbremsen mit Zweikreis-System sind serienmässig.

Das Coupé auf dem Kadett spielt im Opel-Programm die Rolle des flinken, gut ausgestatteten Kleinwagens aus der Grossserie der Bochumer-Werke. Wegen des kurzen Radstands und den hohen Seitenwänden wirkt bei diesem Modell, im Gegensatz zum Rekord, der Coupéaufsatz weniger gut proportioniert, dafür ist der Innenraum gegenüber demjenigen des normalen Kadett kaum wesentlich eingeschränkt. Der Wagenfront hat man durch die quadratische Einfassung der Scheinwerfer und das breit ausgelegte Kühlergitter eine besondere Note verliehen. Für Liebhaber eines völlig normal gebauten, aber mit im Detail verfeinerter konventioneller Radaufhängung versehenen Fahrzeutyps von nur 5 Steuer-PS dürfte der Kadett mit seiner auf 48 PS gesteigerten Motorleistung ein besonderer Anziehungspunkt werden, da Coupés dieser Kategorie auf dem internationalen Markt meist Frontantrieb oder Heckmotor aufweisen, der Kadett aber dank der Normalbauweise einen beträchtlichen Kofferraum bietet.

Respekt vor den grossen Neuheiten

Die absoluten Neuheiten der diesjährigen IAA haben wir unseren Lesern in den vorangegangenen Ausgaben bereits im Detail näher gebracht. In den auf viele Hallen und Pavillons verteilten Monsterausstellung bildeten sie für das Publikum magnetische Anziehungspunkte und die meisten steuerten die Besucher von der Kasse weg zu den ihnen am wichtigsten scheinenden Novitäten, denn für die Deutschen ist die IAA so etwas wie für uns die Mustermesse — ein Stück Nationalstolz.

NEU BEI MERCEDES — Links die Schaltkulisse für den Wählhebel des Getriebeautomaten beim 230 SL, der blitzschnelles und sicheres Schalten gestattet. Rechts die Vorderradscheibenbremse des «Grossen Mercedes» 600 mit je einer Zange vorn und hinten. (Photos «AR»)

NEU AM NSU PRINZ 1000 — Links die abklappbare Rücklehne als Ladefläche. Rechts die Ventiltriebverschalung am neuen luftgekühlten Vierzylindermotor. (Photos Seifert)

Der Grosse Mercedes 600 — Wie unseren Lesern bekannt ist, hat Daimler-Benz, an eine frühere Tradition anknüpfend, jedoch mit dem Elan ihres junggebliebenen Ingenieurteams wieder einen Grossen Mercedes herausgebracht. Er wird in zwei Typen, als Sechsplätzer und als achtsitzige Pulman-Limousine mit vier Seitenfenstern und Trennwand gebaut. Viele Teile dieses Fahrzeuges sind mit denjenigen der kleineren Modelle im Prinzip identisch, in ihrer Ausführung jedoch auf die besonderen Beanspruchungen und Ansprüche denen ein solches Spitzenfahrzeug zu genügen hat, ausgerichtet. Der 6,2-Liter-V8-Motor füllt den im Verhältnis zum Gesamtvolumen des Fahrzeuges nicht übermässig grossen Motorraum zusammen mit den Hilfsmaschinen bis an den Rand aus. Der Motor arbeitet mit intermittierender Benzineinspritzung, er besitzt wie alle Mercedes-Motoren je eine obenliegende Nockenwelle pro Zylinderblock. Für die Kraftübertragung wird der Daimler-Benz-Automat in verstärkter Ausführung verwendet und in der hinteren Pendelachse mit tiefliegendem Drehpunkt ist ein Sperrdifferential eingebaut. Der Grosse Mercedes besitzt reine Luftfederung, die Stossdämpfer können in ihrer Härte vom Lenkrad aus mit einem Hebel reguliert werden. Beachtlich sind die verschiedenen Sicherheitsmassnahmen, wie etwa das Absperrventil in der Luftdruckanlage, das bei einem Defekt an den Federbälgen eine Druckreserve für die Zweikreis-Servobremse zurückbehält, ferner die doppelt ausgeführten Bremszangen an den vorderen Scheibenbremsen, und die Wechselstromgeneratoren in ebenfalls doppelter Ausführung. Im Fahrzeug sind neben einer zentralen hydraulischen Anlage mit der die durch Druckknöpfe gesteuerten Komforteinrichtungen in Gang gesetzt werden (Sitzverstellung, Schiebedach, Lüftungsklappen, Trennscheibe, Türschlösser sowie die Servolenkung) auch eine Druckluftanlage vorhanden an der die Luftfederung mit ihrer Niveauregulierung und die Bremsverstärker angeschlossen sind. Auf Wunsch wird auch eine komplette Klimaanlage mit elektronischer Temperaturregelung (Heizung und Kühlung) eingebaut. Helle Bewunderung erregte beim Publikum die verkehrte Sitzanordnung im Pullman, in dessen Innenraum sich die Passagiere wie schon um die Jahrhundertwende im Benz-Vis-à-Vis-Drahtspeichenwagen gegenüber sitzen. Berufschauffeure betrachteten die knappen Längsmasse des Führersitzes etwas skeptisch, wohl nicht wissend, dass die Länge der Lenksäule durch Hydraulik dem Bauchumfang angepasst werden kann. Man kann sich von diesem monumentalen Ausstellungsobjekt nicht leicht trennen, glaubt doch jeder irgend eines der 1000 Details vielleicht doch noch übersehen zu haben. Als Richtpreise wurden genannt: für den Sechsplätzer 49 000 DM und für die Pullman-Limousine 56 000 DM. Pro kg Leergewicht sind das für den Sechsplätzer DM 18.75 gegenüber DM 6.82 beim VW 1500...

BMW 1800 TI — Im Innern des BMW 1800 TI wurde eine Mittelkonsole aufgebaut, die ein Ablagefach enthält.

NSU-Spider mit Wankel-Kreiskolbenmotor. — Der kleine rote Spider in der italienischen Linienführung von Bertone auf dem schwerbefrachteten NSU-Stand hat der Halle 1a einen Massenzustrom gebracht. Das Interesse galt natürlich weniger dem hübschen zweiplätzigen Cabriolet, das vom Sport Prinz abgeleitet ist, als vielmehr dem im Heck unter dem Kofferboden eingebauten Wankel-Motor. Man bestaunte die vielen Nebenaggregate, wie etwa den Solex-Spezialvergaser, den seitlichen Wärmeaustauscher, der die Rückkühlung des Motoröles im Kühlwasserstrom besorgt, die konventionelle elektrische Anlage, die einzige vorhandene Zündkerze und die grosse verrippte Oelwanne unter dem Motorgehäuse. Das eigentliche Kreiskolbengehäuse, in welchem aus 500 cm³ Kammervolumen 50 PS bei 4000 U/min erzeugt werden, war als solches nicht leicht zu erkennen, es lag unter der Kühlwasserzu-

Fortsetzung Seite 21

PORSCHE-SECHSZYLINDERMOTOR — Im neuen Modell 901 verwendet Porsche einen luftgekühlten Sechszylinder-Boxermotor mit kurzem Hub. Die Hauptdaten lauten: Mit Ketten angetriebene obenliegende Nockenwelle pro Zylinderblock, Leichtmetallkurbelgehäuse, Graugusszylinder, Leichtmetallzylinderköpfe, 8 Kurbelwellenlager, Verdichtung 9:1, 130 PS bei 6200 U/min, max. Drehmoment 16,5 mkg bei 4600 U/min.

Kraftstrotzender Ford Mustang «Tour de France»

(Schluss von Seite 19)

leistung des grossen V8 auf den Boden zu bringen.

Das Fahrverhalten des rennsportlich gezüchteten Mustang kann als beinahe *völlig neutral* bezeichnet werden. Er reagiert positiv auf die Intentionen des Fahrers, wenn auch die Wirkung des *Sperrdifferentials* als hart empfunden wird. Immerhin verlangt auch der leistungsstarke Mustang die volle Aufmerksamkeit des Fahrers, wenn es gilt Kurven im Rennstil zu fahren. Man gewöhnt sich vom Lenkrad aus relativ rasch an die Besonderheiten dieses schnellen Mustang-Exemplars. Nach einem Tag Fahrpraxis vermag man bereits die Vorteile seiner Wendigkeit beim Kurvenfahren voll auszunützen. Man gewinnt Vertrauen in die Sicherheit. Die *Goodyear-Spezialreifen* beeinflussen keineswegs die Leichtgängigkeit der Lenkung, sie sind für den Fahrer nicht ermüdend.

Wenn auch der Mustang in der geprüften Ausführung ein reines Wettbewerbsfahrzeug darstellt, so war er dennoch im dichtesten Verkehr leicht zu beherrschen und refüsierte nie vor den Hindernissen des Stadtverkehrs. *Durch den Motorlärm zieht er natürlich viele Blicke auf sich.* Die im Stadtverkehr eintretende Motorerhitzung lässt allerdings den Schluss zu, dass sich dieser Mustang hier nicht in seinem Element befindet, er liebt die freien Strassen weit mehr.

Abzug wie ein Dragster

Die hohe Motorleistung und die vollkommene Art, mit der sie dank dem Sperrdifferential und den Spezialreifen auf den Boden gebracht wird, ergeben für den Mustang phantastische Beschleunigungszeiten. Sie stehen denjenigen der schnellsten Gran-Turismo-Wagen nicht nach und gemahnen an den Anriss der bei den Amerikanern so beliebten Dragster, die nur aus einem riesigen Motor in einem leichten Chassis bestehen.

In 7,5 sec wird die 100-km/h-Marke vom Start weg erreicht, in 18,8 sec kommt er auf 160 km/h. Den stehenden Kilometer legte der Mustang in 27,2 sec zurück, wobei er die ersten 400 m in 15,2 sec hinter sich brachte. 230 km/h Spitze sind bestimmt kein schlechtes Ergebnis für einen kompakten Tourenwagen. Die Fahrstabilität ist auch bei Höchstgeschwindigkeit noch voll erhalten, wenn auch die sichere Beherrschung des Wagens, vor allem auf nicht seidenglatter Fahrbahn, einige Konzentration verlangt.

Abgesehen vom 1. Gang, der mit einer Spitze von 105 km/h etwas lang erscheint, ist die Abstufung der übrigen drei Gänge korrekt. Der 2. Gang reicht bis 150 km/h, der dritte bis 185 km/h, und im vierten scheint es unter allergünstigsten Bedingungen möglich, die in den Probeläufen erreichten 230 km/h noch zu überschreiten.

Die ausgezeichnet arbeitenden Bremsen, die sichere Strassenlage und die aussergewöhnlichen Beschleunigungszeiten machen den Erfolg des Ford Mustang an der Tour de France leicht erklärlich. Selbst bei sehr intensiver Beanspruchung der Bremsen zeigten sie keine Tendenz zum Fading, die einzige Auswirkung der Ueberhitzung bestand darin, dass sich der Pedalweg etwas verlängerte. Nachdem nun auch die nicht frisierten Mustang 1965 mit vorderen Scheibenbremsen ausgerüstet sind, darf man von diesen Normalmodellen ähnliche Bremsqualitäten erwarten.

Wenn auch der geprüfte Mustang sich ziemlich stark vom Serienmodell entfernt, so war doch beachtlich, dass dieses Exemplar trotz der an der Tour de France ausgestandenen Beanspruchung nichts von seinem Brio eingebüsst hatte. Man darf erwarten, dass er auch in der Saison 1965 noch von sich reden machen wird.

IMPOSANTER V8-MOTOR — Den im Mustang Tour de France eingebauten 4,7-Liter-V8 findet man auch im AC Cobra. Mit Vierfachvergaser leistet er 285 DIN-PS und verleiht dem Wagen aussergewöhnliche Fahrleistungen. (Photos B. Cahier)

Porsche 911 aus der Serie

(Schluss von Seite 17)

tere Sicht insbesondere nach vorne und nach rückwärts. Ausserdem verfügt der 911 nunmehr über einen veritablen *Gepäckraum*, der zwei grosse Koffern aufnimmt. Dieses Merkmal trägt weiter dazu bei, den 911 unter die echten 2 + 2plätzigen Coupés einzureihen.

Die Radaufhängung vorn weicht prinzipiell von derjenigen des Modells 356 ab. Die Räder werden an untern Querlenkern, senkrechten Teleskopstossdämpfern und längsliegenden Torsionsstabfedern geführt und gefedert (der 356 besitzt eine Kurbelachse mit Quertorsionsstäben). Sämtliche Räder sind mit Scheibenbremsen ausgerüstet.

Ein GT auf hohem Niveau

Die erste Ueberraschung bei laufendem Motor ist akustischer Natur. Das Motorgeräusch hat nicht mehr viel gemeinsam mit den typischen Paukenschlägen des Vierzylinders; es erinnert mehr an den rauschenden Chevrolet-Corvair-Motor. Auf den ersten Fahrkilometern begegnet der Porsche-Kenner drei weiteren Besonderheiten: Der Wagen ist bei aller Sportlichkeit weicher, gefälliger geworden; die Verfeinerung ist deutlich betont und der Fahrkomfort ausgeprägter. Der 911 besitzt somit Qualitäten, die man nur bei Wagen mit grösserem Zylinderinhalt und in einer höheren Preisklasse vorfindet.

Die Handhabung des *Schalthebels* erfordert zunächst einige Angewöhnung beim Wechseln vom ersten in den zweiten Gang, zumal man, bei kräftigem Zupacken unversehens in den dritten Gang gerät. Dies lässt sich vermeiden, wenn man den Hebel seinen Weg selber suchen lässt und nur mit leichter Handbewegung nachhilft. Wenn man den Trick los hat, erweist sich das Porsche-Vollsynchrongetriebe als sehr befriedigend.

Der Wagen ist zu hohen Fahrleistungen prädestiniert und täuscht sehr über die verwirklichten hohen *Geschwindigkeiten*; man ist gehalten, anhand der Instrumente seine Fahrweise zu überwachen. Im niedrigen Drehzahlbereich ist der Motor laut; man hört das Arbeiten des Kühlluftgebläses; mit zunehmender Drehzahl wird er indessen immer angenehmer, und zwischen 3000 und 7000 U/min ist keine merkliche Geräuschzunahme festzustellen.

Mit *drei* Lenkradumdrehungen von Anschlag zu Anschlag hat man jetzt gegenüber dem Prototyp einen Kompromiss gefunden, der angenehmes und präzises Lenken vereint.

Wenn auch der Motor im hintern Ueberhang untergebracht ist und demzufolge eine Hecklastigkeit zu erwarten wäre, so trifft diese Befürchtung nicht zu; im Gegenteil, die Strassenlage ist schlechthin phantastisch. Der Wagen verhält sich in Kurven fast neutral, mit einer leichten Tendenz zum Untersteuern bei sportlicher Fahrweise. Auf trockenen und nassen Strassen resultiert daraus ein untrügliches Sicherheitsgefühl, wenn auch der Wagen gegenüber verschiedenen Strassenoberflächen nicht ganz indifferent ist. Auf Seitenwind ist der 911 wenig empfindlich. Gegenüber dem Modell 365 stellt er einen beachtlichen Fortschritt dar; dieser fällt um so mehr auf, als die Federung sehr komfortabel ist und die Karosserie trotzdem bei scharfer Fahrt nur ganz wenig Seitenneigung aufkommen lässt.

Mit geringem Pedaldruck erreicht man bereits kräftige *Bremsverzögerungen;* dies ist um so auffallender, als kein Servoapparat beim Bremsen mithilft. Auf nassen Strassen muss man mit diesen zugriffigen Bremsen vorsichtig umgehen. Im übrigen besitzen sie jene Qualität, die man bei einem schnellen Fahrzeug verlangen muss.

Die *Gaspedalbedienung* ist, gemessen an den übrigen Bedienungsfeinheiten, überraschend schwergängig. Man hat wenig Spielfreiheit am Pedal; jedes Zurücknehmen erzeugt spürbaren Leistungsrückgang.

Die im Kurztest gemessenen Beschleunigungszeiten bewegen sich in der Nähe derjenigen des Ferrari 2+2. Für den stehenden Kilometer wurden 29,5 sec, für die ersten 400 m 16,6 sec registriert. Unter günstigen Bedingungen dürfte die Spitze von 209 km/h noch zu überschreiten sein. Hält man sich an eine Drehzahl von 6500 U/min (Höchstleistung bei 7000 U/min), so erreicht man vom 1. bis 4. Gang folgende Geschwindigkeiten: 60, 101, 153, 180 km/h. Das Fünfganggetriebe erleichtert das Erreichen hoher Durchschnitte selbst auf Strassen unterschiedlicher Qualität. Zwischen dem 4. und 5. Gang besteht nur ein Drehzahlunterschied von 500 U/min. Man kann aber im Schnellgang das Tempo bis auf 2000 U/min sinken lassen, so elastisch arbeitet der Sechszylinder. Bei 160 km/h Reisegeschwindigkeit arbeitet der Motor im 5. Gang nur mit 6000 U/min.

Gesamteindruck: Mit viel Esprit entworfen, von profiliertem Charakter, sicher, schnell und komfortabel, vermag der 911 die Wünsche der Liebhaber eines 2+2-Coupés von kompakten Abmessungen, luxuriöser Ausstattung und hohen Fahrleistungen zu erfüllen. Der 911 dürfte auch jenen Enthusiasten gefallen, die vielleicht das wütende Bellen und die Angriffsluft des Carrera-Vierzylinders im 911 vermissen.

Bernhard Cahier

MIRACLES NEVER CEASE

HENCE THERE ARE EVEN A COUPLE OF SURVIVING 901s

A few 901s have actually survived the decades – some were well looked after, others stood (like the red one) for decades, buried in the undergrowth in the American Mid-West.

ALOIS RUF IS RESTORING EVEN THIS 901 WRECK TO A PERFECT 901 – LIKE THE BLUE ONE NEXT TO IT.

WITH *PERFECT* CRAFTSMANSHIP, EVEN APPARENTLY *HOPELESS* RUINS CAN BE RESURRECTED

THE INTERIOR EXUDES 46 YEARS OF HISTORY.

THE MORBID CHARM OF DECAY IS APPARENT.

SHOULD A
CONTEMPORARY
ARTEFACT
OF THIS KIND
ACTUALLY BE
RESTORED?

UNITED AS ONE FOR DECADES — IGNITION KEY AND 901.   SILENT FOR YEARS — THE TWO-LITER SIX-CYLINDER.

PAGE 169

PAGE 170

AFTER A TWO-YEAR RESTORATION
AT ALOIS RUF, THE 901 WITH
CHASSIS NUMBER 300027 LIVES
ONCE MORE.

A 901 WITH A VERY SPECIAL HISTORY – IT WAS BOUGHT IN OCTOBER 1964 FROM THE STAND AT THE
EARLS COURT MOTOR SHOW IN LONDON BY A YOUNG FINNISH ENGINEER, WHO HAS KEPT THE CAR TO THIS
DAY. AFTER 46 YEARS, NUMBER 27 HAS BEEN RESTORED FOR THE FIRST TIME.

DEVELOPMENT STORIES ALWAYS THROW UP SURPRISES – THE 901 WITH CHASSIS NUMBER 300049 IS ACTUALLY THE FIRST OFFICIAL 911. TODAY, THE UR-911 BELONGS TO AMERICAN ACTOR, COMEDIAN AND AUTHOR JERRY SEINFELD.

PAGE 173

ACKNOWLEDGEMENTS

This book would not have been possible without the generous and intensive support of Dr. Wolfgang Porsche, as well as the press department and archive of Dr. Ing. h.c. F. Porsche AG in Stuttgart. Special thanks goes here to Dieter Landenberger and Jens Torner, who not only improved this book with all of their suggestions, but also found all sorts of new documents hidden in the depths of the archive and read through the text in great depth – thank you very much for your support. It was also a pleasure to spend a great deal of time with Jörg Austen, Karl Bareis, Paul Hensler, Gerhard W. E. Höfig, Herbert Linge, Hans Mezger, Dr. Heinz Rabe, Lars R. Schmidt and Harald Wagner, who have so much to tell about the times back then that I could easily fill several more books.

Alois Ruf provided not only his immaculate 901 for a photo shoot at the René Staud Studios – he also patiently explained the secrets of the early 901, of which he restored the majority at his company in Pfaffenhausen. René Staud photographed yet another car for one of my books – dear René, thank you for your many years of friendship.

This book should not and cannot replace any of the works by Tobias Aichele, Paul Frère and Karl Ludvigsen – these books are the basis of the 911 legend. I have, however, endeavored to tell the story of the birth of the legend from another angle – to describe the long, difficult labor and the internal difficulties.

Last but not least, I would like to thank Konrad Delius and Edwin Baaske at Delius Klasing – after all these years, it is still a pleasure to work with this publisher and its people.

Author and publisher thank:

Dr. Wolfgang Porsche, Chairman of the Supervisory Board,

Dr. Ing. h.c. F. Porsche AG

Hans-Gerd Bode

Achim Stejskal

Dieter Landenberger

Jens Torner

Tobias Aichele

Jörg Austen

Karl Bareis

Uwe Biegner

Wolfgang Blaube

Christian Dau

Norbert Grabotin

Fritz Haberlt (†)

Paul Hensler

Gerhard W. E. Höfig

Wolfgang Karger

Herbert Linge

Hans Mezger

Matthias Pfannmüller

Dr. Heinz Rabe

Urs Paul Ramseier

Lars R. Schmidt

Harald Wagner

Alois Ruf, RUF Automobile, Pfaffenhausen (D)

René Staud, René Staud Studios, Leonberg (D)

Magazines:

Automobile Quarterly

Der Spiegel (D)

Motor Revue, Motor Presse Verlag, Stuttgart (D)

auto motor und sport, Motor Presse Verlag, Stuttgart (D)

Automobil Revue, Bern (CH)

Bibliography:

Tobias Aichele, *Porsche 911 – Forever Young*,
Motorbuch Verlag, Stuttgart (D) 1994

Tobias Aichele, *Porsche Raritäten*,
GeraMond Verlag, München (D) 2009

Paul Frère, *Die Porsche 911 Story*,
Motorbuch Verlag, Stuttgart (D) 2007

Albrecht Graf Goertz, *You've got to be lucky*,
author's publisher, 2002

Karl Ludvigsen, *Excellence was Expected*, Bentley Publishers,
Cambridge MA (USA) 1997; German edition: *Perfektion ist
selbstverständlich*, Heel Verlag, Königswinter (D) 2008

Ferdinand Piëch, *Auto.Biographie*,
Hoffmann & Campe, Hamburg (D) 2002

Ferry Porsche/Günther Molter, *Ferry Porsche – ein Leben für
das Auto*, Motorbuch Verlag, Stuttgart (D) 1989

German Library bibliographical information
The German Library has recorded this publication
in the German National Bibliography. Detailed bibliographical
information is available at http://dnb.dnb.de.

This book was published in Germany 2010 and 2012 under its
original title *Porsche 901 – Die Wurzeln einer Legende*

First edition in English
ISBN 978-3-7688-3663-0
© by Delius, Klasing & Co. KG, Bielefeld (D)

Idea and concept: Jürgen Lewandowski
Editorial collaboration: Monika Lewandowski
Translation: Elaine Catton
Editing: Joachim Fischer, Alexander Failing
Project management: Marco Brinkmann, Florian Strob
Art Direction: Weusthoff Noël, Hamburg (D)
Lithography: scanlitho.teams, Bielefeld (D)
Printed by: Firmengruppe APPL – aprinta druck, Wemding
Printed in Germany 2013

Delius Klasing Verlag, Siekerwall 21, D - 33602 Bielefeld
Telephone +49 521 55 90, Telefax +49 521 55 91 15
E-mail info@delius-klasing.de
www.delius-klasing.de